Distracted Driving

by Toney Allman

LUCENT BOOKS

A part of Gale, Cengage Learning

Farmington Hills, Mich • San Francisco • New York • Waterville, Maine
Meriden, Conn • Mason, Ohio • Chicago

LIBRARY OF CONGRESS CATALOGING-IN-PUBLICATION DATA

Allman, Toney.
  Distracted driving / by Toney Allman.
    pages cm. -- (Hot topics)
  Includes bibliographical references and index.
  ISBN 978-1-4205-1233-5 (hardcover)
  1. Distracted driving--United States--Juvenile literature. 2. Traffic safety--United States--Juvenile literature. I. Title.
  HE5620.D59A45 2015
  362.12'51--dc23
                                    2014031008

Lucent Books
27500 Drake Rd.
Farmington Hills, MI 48331

ISBN-13: 978-1-4205-1233-5
ISBN-10: 1-4205-1233-1

Printed in the United States of America
1 2 3 4 5 6 7 18 17 16 15 14

CONTENTS

FOREWORD

Young people today are bombarded with information. Aside from traditional sources such as newspapers, television, and the radio, they are inundated with a nearly continuous stream of data from electronic media. They send and receive e-mails and instant messages, read and write online blogs, participate in chat rooms and forums, and surf the web for hours. This trend is likely to continue. As Patricia Senn Breivik, the former dean of university libraries at Wayne State University in Detroit, has stated, "Information overload will only increase in the future. By 2020, for example, the available body of information is expected to double every 73 days! How will these students find the information they need in this coming tidal wave of information?"

Ironically, this overabundance of information can actually impede efforts to understand complex issues. Whether the topic is abortion, the death penalty, gay rights, or obesity, the deluge of fact and opinion that floods the print and electronic media is overwhelming. The news media report the results of polls and studies that contradict one another. Cable news shows, talk radio programs, and newspaper editorials promote narrow viewpoints and omit facts that challenge their own political biases. The World Wide Web is an electronic minefield where legitimate scholars compete with the postings of ordinary citizens who may or may not be well informed or capable of reasoned argument. At times, strongly worded testimonials and opinion pieces both in print and electronic media are presented as factual accounts.

Conflicting quotes and statistics can confuse even the most diligent researchers. A good example of this is the question of whether or not the death penalty deters crime. For instance, one study found that murders decreased by nearly one-third when the death penalty was reinstated in New York in 1995. Death penalty supporters cite this finding to support their argument that the existence of the death penalty deters criminals from committing murder. However, another study found that states without the death penalty have murder rates below the national average. This study is cited by opponents of capital punishment, who reject the claim that the death penalty deters murder. Students need context and clear, informed discussion if they are to think critically and make informed decisions.

The Hot Topics series is designed to help young people wade through the glut of fact, opinion, and rhetoric so that they can think critically about controversial issues. Only by reading and thinking critically will they be able to formulate a viewpoint that is not simply the parroted views of others. Each volume of the series focuses on one of today's most pressing social issues and provides a balanced overview of the topic. Carefully crafted narrative, fully documented primary and secondary source quotes, informative sidebars, and study questions all provide excellent starting points for research and discussion. Full-color photographs and charts enhance all volumes in the series. With its many useful features, the Hot Topics series is a valuable resource for young people struggling to understand the pressing issues of the modern era.

INTRODUCTION

A DEADLY EPIDEMIC

In 2010, then U.S. Department of Transportation secretary Ray LaHood declared his determination to fight what he called the epidemic of distracted driving on America's roadways. He said, "Distracted driving-related crashes killed nearly 5,500 people in 2009 and injured almost half a million more. Lives are at stake, and all the reputable research we have says that tough laws, good enforcement and increased public awareness will help put a stop to the deadly epidemic of distracted driving on our roads." He vehemently added, "When it comes to safety, I will take a back-seat to no one. I am going to continue working to put an end to the deadly epidemic of distracted driving, in addition to tackling the other safety challenges we face on our nation's roads."[1]

Still, the Epidemic Goes On

Today, despite extensive efforts, the challenge remains as large as it was in 2010, if not larger. Distracted driving continues to be an epidemic problem. In 2014, for example, the police chief in New Canaan, Connecticut—Leon Krolikowski—echoed La-Hood's words when he labeled distracted driving the "new traffic safety epidemic" in his city. In a newspaper column, he argued, in part, "Drivers simply do not realize—or choose to ignore— the danger they create when they take their eyes off the road, their hands off the wheel, and their focus off driving. Distracted driving is the most significant threat to traffic safety we have seen in many years."[2]

Krolikowski is most concerned about the highly visible and serious distractions caused by the use of electronic devices, such as cell phones, but he warns that any activity that takes a person's focus off driving is distracting and dangerous. He asks all drivers to commit to driving free of distractions, to urge friends and family members to drive distraction-free, and even to be a responsible passenger and object if the driver is being distracted. The Department of Transportation's website, Distraction.gov, offers the same good advice, but too often the information is ignored by too many people in the United States and around the world. Many experts wonder what it will take to convince drivers that distractions are hazardous and even deadly.

Distractions of just one or two seconds can cause devastating accidents.

Real-Life Consequences

Caitlin Hommerson learned how driving distracted can change lives and even kill when she was just eighteen years old. Early one morning in 2012, Caitlin and her sixteen-year-old sister, Andi, were driving to school in Monroe, Michigan. As Caitlin turned a corner, her water bottle slipped from the center console of the car and dropped to the floor. Caitlin was distracted for two or three seconds at most as she leaned over to pick up the bottle. Her hand left the steering wheel and her eyes left the road. In that short amount of time, Caitlin steered the car off the road and into a mailbox at the curb. Standing beside the mailbox, in her own driveway, was a mother, Shelly Deaton, who was watching her daughter Desirae walk to the school bus. Caitlin could not stop. Her car crashed into Deaton and killed her as Desirae watched.

The tragic accident damaged two families that day. A teenage girl's mother was lost. Another teen faced the awful knowledge that she had taken the life of a beloved human being. Caitlin also had to deal with the legal consequences of her distracted driving. She feared going to prison, and although that did not happen, she did find herself involved with the courts. She was placed on probation, had her license suspended, and was fined. She also needed to see a counselor to cope with her own devastated emotions. Deaton's family forgave Caitlin, knowing how sorry she was. Deaton's father, Bill, even comforted the sobbing Caitlin in court. A year later, a still-traumatized Caitlin was so grateful for Bill's forgiveness. She said, "He's giving me the okay to live on. It means the whole world to me."[3]

Caitlin wants to share her story with other teens, and she has one important reason for doing so. She explains, "I'm trying to convey a message. You can't be distracted while driving."[4] It is a message that everyone needs to hear.

WHAT IS DISTRACTED DRIVING?

In June 2008, twenty-year-old Pennsylvania resident Amanda Kloehr was serving in the U.S. Air Force at McGuire Air Force Base in New Jersey. She decided to take a driving trip to Newport News, Virginia, to visit a friend. She was on Route 13, near Norfolk, Virginia, when the accident happened. Kloehr slammed into the back of a tractor-trailer. The car slid underneath the huge truck and was crushed flat. Pinned inside with her face smashed and a piece of the tractor-trailer's engine impaling her leg, Kloehr could not stop screaming. She remembers the pain, but cannot remember how the accident happened or exactly what she was doing when she hit the tractor-trailer, which she did not even see, as it waited in her lane to make a left-hand turn ahead of her. She knows, however, that the terrible crash was her fault. She says, "I do not remember the impact at all. I was distracted. I had my GPS and my cell phone."[5] Kloehr paid a heavy price for her inattentiveness at the wheel. She was in the hospital for a month, had multiple reconstructive surgeries on her crushed face, spent a year learning to walk all over again, and lost an eye.

Today, Kloehr is fully recovered from her injuries, and is on a mission. She spends much of her time traveling the country and talking to groups of young people about the dangers of distracted driving. During her speeches, she shows the audience the scars on her face and her prosthetic eye. Then, she says, "This is what lucky looks like. I'm still here, and I didn't kill anyone. I want you to think about it and look at it. This could be you or the person you hit because you thought that text message or phone call was more important than paying attention to the road."[6]

How Distraction Works

No one will ever know whether Amanda Kloehr took her eyes off the road to look at her cell phone or adjust the radio buttons in the car or to check her GPS, but it does not really matter what she was doing. Her experience was an example of distracted driving—a behavior that puts millions of people at risk each and every day around the world. The U.S. Department of Transportation's National Highway Traffic Safety Administration (NHTSA) explains, "Distracted driving is any activity that could divert a person's attention away from the primary task of driving. *All* distractions endanger driver, passenger, and bystander safety."[7]

DRIVING IS NOT SIMPLE

"Driving a car is a very complex task. It requires your complete attention. All it takes is a glance away for more than two seconds and you can get into serious trouble."—Barbara Harsha, executive director of the Governors Highway Safety Association

Quoted in Teddi Dineley Johnson. "Distracted driving: Stay focused when on the road." *The Nation's Health*, February 2012. http://thenationshealth.aphapublications.org/content/42/1/28.full.

The NHTSA identifies three major types of distraction that can occur while driving. They are visual, manual, and cognitive. Visual distraction is taking one's eyes off the road. When a parent, for instance, glances over at a child to be sure his or her seat belt is fastened or a driver looks at a field of cows in the distance, it is a visual distraction. Some scientific studies suggest that electronic billboards posted along the highways are visual distractions that are hard for drivers to resist. These digital billboards are brighter than regular billboards and road signs and

constantly flash different, changing advertisements that draw a driver's eyes away from the road. In 2013, the Swedish National Road and Transport Research Institute studied forty-one different drivers and their visual reactions as they drove past both standard and digital billboards. The researchers discovered that the drivers stared at the electronic billboards longer than they did other road signs. The researchers reported such a strong visual distraction that the Swedish government banned electronic billboards as likely to increase automobile accidents.

Manual distraction is taking one's hands off the steering wheel. A manually distracted driver might remove a hand from the steering wheel to scratch his or her neck or to reach for a cup in the car's center console. Massachusetts resident Joan Jaeger reports a common example of manually distracted driving that she has engaged in herself. She says she often eats when she is driving, as do many people. Usually, Jaeger eats with just one hand, keeping the other hand on the steering wheel. She admits, however, "Once in a while, I would get a Frosty and that you just have to eat with a spoon! Knees come in handy then . . . one hand for the cup, one hand for the spoon, and the knees for the steering wheel."[8] Whether or not she is aware of it, she is describing manually distracted driving that could endanger herself and others. Driving with only one hand on the wheel is a manual distraction, and driving with both hands off the wheel is perhaps the most serious of manual distractions.

Cognitive distraction is taking one's mind or mental attention off the task of driving. Cognitive or mental distractions involve losing one's focus on driving. Such a distracted driver might be daydreaming, thinking about what to wear to a party, or worrying about an argument with a friend or family member. Cognitive distractions do not have to be stressful or negative to be dangerous. For example, in 2011, a Canadian bus driver was not paying attention to his job because he was daydreaming about the upcoming Christmas holiday. He was so lost in thought that he started up his bus from a bus stop before an exiting passenger had cleared the rear doors. The passenger, an eighty-four-year-old man, fell down the steps and under the bus, and the bus' wheels ran over his legs. The injured man spent more than three months recovering in the hospital, and eventually one of his legs had to be amputated. The bus driver, Veraldin Ong, felt terrible about the accident. He said, "I did not deliberately do these things. I'm an honest person . . . If I could take back time, I would."[9] Ong was not an uncaring or deliberately negligent driver, but his cognitive distraction had serious consequences.

Multiple Types of Distractions

Some activities that people engage in while driving may involve only one type of distraction, but some may involve two or all three types of distractions at the same time. For example, a driver adjusting the car radio may glance down at the radio while using one hand to adjust the volume. This is an instance of both

Eating while driving is a common distraction that can lead to accidents.

manual and visual distraction. Eating while driving also may involve multiple types of distractions. For example, a Massachusetts woman named Helen Cymbala says that she once choked
on a chunk of meat that she was eating while driving on the

highway. Her distractions were not just manual, but also cognitive and visual, as she worked to recover from the momentary incident. She did not have an accident, but she was frightened and did learn from the experience not to eat such food on her road trips. Janie Garza, a Washington State driver, knows that eating behind the wheel involves multiple distractions, even though she—like about 70 percent of all drivers—admits that she has eaten while driving. She says, "If I'm eating something and it just falls, like a taco, it's just messy and falls in my lap, I kind of panic more than watching the road."[10]

Texting while driving may be the most obvious example of behavior that always involves all three types of distractions. When a driver sends or receives a text message, he or she must look or glance repeatedly at the smartphone, use at least one hand to hold the phone or type the text message, and almost always think about what is being read or written. One young man who reports texting regularly says, "I put the phone on top of the steering wheel and text with both thumbs."[11] Obviously, he also has to look at what he is texting and think about what he is saying. Thus, the behavior is visually, manually, and cognitively distracting. In 2009, researchers at the Virginia Tech Transportation Institute conducted the first real-life study of the dangers of texting and driving by placing video cameras in the cabs of long-distance truck drivers. The truckers were videoed whenever they were driving, whether they were texting or not. After eighteen months, the researchers looked at the data, including any accidents in which the trucks were involved. They discovered that texting greatly increased the chance of an accident. Truckers who sent text messages while driving increased the risk of an accident 23 times over their risk when no distractions were involved.

Other distractions that can involve multiple types of inattention include e-mailing, reading a map, using a cell phone to make or receive calls, checking a GPS or navigational system, looking at a video, grooming (putting on makeup or combing hair, for example), and talking with passengers. Even listening to

Drowsy Driving

Drowsy driving is driving while fatigued, sleepy, or tired, or actually falling asleep at the wheel, and it is just as dangerous as distracted driving or drunk driving. Identifying drowsy driving at an accident scene is difficult, but the National Highway Traffic Safety Administration (NHTSA) estimates that 2.5 percent of fatal crashes and 2 percent of injury crashes involve drowsy driving. In addition, NHTSA reports a 2009–2010 survey in which 4.2 percent of respondents admitted to falling asleep while driving in the past thirty days. Drowsiness is extremely dangerous because it slows reaction times, makes drivers inattentive, and reduces a driver's ability to make quick decisions. Drowsiness can be an especial problem for people who drive long distances, people who work night shifts, people who take prescription or over-the-counter medications, and people who are sleep-deprived and do not get enough sleep. NHTSA lists some of the warning signs of drowsiness as frequent yawning, drifting from one's lane, frequent blinking, and trouble remembering the last few miles driven. It recommends that drivers who experience any warning signs should pull over or change drivers. Such tactics as eating, opening the window, or turning on the radio do not work to maintain alertness.

music on a radio or MP3 player can be a distraction if the driver drifts off into concentrating on the song instead of the road. That would be a cognitive distraction, but in 2014, New Jersey ambulance driver Jonathan Williams was recorded on his dashboard camera responding to music with multiple inattentive activities. He was listening to Rihanna's "Pour It Up" and began dancing in his seat while driving. He waved his arms and shook his legs in time to the music. His hands left the steering wheel, and he could barely keep his foot on the gas pedal. His eyes momentarily but frequently left the road. People enjoyed watching the video of his antics on television and the Internet, but his driving and dancing really was not funny. It was an example of distracted driving. Many people criticized him, and his employer reprimanded him for dangerous driving behavior.

Distractions and Danger

Distracted driving is no laughing matter, even though every driver has been guilty of it at one time or another. According to Distraction.gov, the U.S. government's official website on distracted driving, 3,328 American people were killed in traffic accidents involving distracted drivers in 2012 (the latest year for which statistics are available). In that same year, an additional estimated 421,000 people were injured in distraction-related vehicle accidents.

As long ago as 2006, researchers and safety experts knew that distracted driving was an important risk factor for traffic accidents, whether or not anyone was injured or killed. A Virginia Tech study at that time estimated that eight out of every ten crashes and near-crashes were due to driver distraction and inattention. The researchers arrived at the 80 percent estimate by placing video cameras and monitors in the cars of more than two hundred drivers for more than a year. The cameras were aimed at the driver's face, the steering wheel, and the front and rear of each vehicle. They showed what the drivers were doing as they

Many people do not realize how dangerous a simple distraction such as applying lipstick can be.

traveled and what was happening in the moments before a crash or a near-miss. In all, the researchers had 43,300 hours of data on driver behavior to analyze for 2 million miles of driving. They saw 82 crashes and 761 near-accidents. The scientists were surprised at what they saw people doing as they drove along. They were applying lipstick, tuning radios and MP3 players, turning to look out driver-side windows, drinking coffee, and even reading newspapers. One woman was spotted driving with her knees while she was playing her flute. About 10 percent of drivers were distracted by cell phone use—dialing, talking, reading e-mails, or checking the Internet. Virginia Tech researcher Charlie Klauer said at the time, "All of these activities are much more dangerous than we thought before."[12]

Distracting Devices

Today, the Virginia Tech Transportation Institute reports that the use of handheld electronic devices has become the most common distraction for all drivers. According to the U.S. Centers for Disease Control and Prevention (CDC), 69 percent of drivers between the ages of eighteen and sixty-four report that they have used a cell phone while driving. In one survey, about 31 percent of American drivers admit to sending or receiving texts within the last thirty days of the poll. The percentage of drivers who report e-mailing or texting rises for teens. Almost half of these drivers say that they will text or e-mail while driving. Using electronic devices is a problem in other countries, too, although it is not as common as in the United States. The CDC reports that 21 percent of drivers in the United Kingdom use cell phones while driving. In Portugal, the number is 59 percent; in Spain and France, it is 40 percent; and in Germany, it is 39 percent. In the Canadian province of Alberta, researchers at the University of Alberta reported in 2011 that 52 percent of drivers used cell phones while driving.

As the use of electronic devices has exploded, distracted driving has become the number-one cause of fatal crashes in the Canadian province of Nova Scotia. In Ontario, Canada, police statistics reveal that distracted driving has passed intoxicated driving as a cause of vehicle accidents and is responsible for at least 30 percent of all accidents there. Even that percentage may be too low. Tim Baillie, a firefighter in British Columbia, explains that statistics probably underestimate the number of crashes caused by distracted driving and especially cell phone use. He tells about a terrible accident he responded to as an example. The car, carrying three young people, had left a straight stretch of road, run into a ditch, and skidded until it hit a driveway. The young people were thrown from the car. Baillie says, "There was no reason why this vehicle should've gone off the road. Can you say that was a distracted driver? You can't prove it, just like

Electronic devices can cause visual, manual, and cognitive distractions for a driver.

an awful lot of the stats that deal with distracted driving." But Baillie suspects that a cell phone was to blame. He adds, "Ever since those damned things came in, there's been distractions. It's getting worse and worse and worse."[13]

The Modern Driving Dilemma

"Calls came in as I drove. Most of the time, I could answer simply by tapping a button on the wheel, but on occasion the call would get routed to my phone, forcing me to dig into my pockets, or ignore the call. And who does that?"—News columnist Peter Cheney

Peter Cheney. "When Will Distracted Driving Be as Unacceptable as Driving Drunk?" *Globe and Mail*, February 5, 2014. www.theglobeandmail.com/globe-drive/culture/commuting /when-will-distracted-driving-be-as-unacceptable-as-driving-drunk/article16707865.

Any distraction increases the risk of an accident or near-accident, but statistics about the different inattentive behaviors that can cause crashes are never completely accurate, because distractions can be hard to prove. When inattention causes only a near-accident, authorities never have a record of the incident at all. That is why estimates of accidents caused by distracted driving range from a low of 25 percent to 80 percent or more. Nevertheless, the use of electronic devices while driving can at least be estimated and often proved when an accident occurs. Therefore, scientists and transportation experts have some evidence about the effects of these kinds of distractions. Distraction.gov estimates that at any given moment during daylight hours, each and every day, 660,000 U.S. drivers are using some kind of electronic device. Every day, estimates the CDC, 9 people are killed and 1,060 people are injured in vehicle accidents involving a distracted driver. Any kind of distraction, reports the Insurance Bureau of Canada, causes driver impairment— the inability to react to a potentially dangerous situation that is equal to that of an intoxicated driver with a blood alcohol level of .08 (the legal definition of drunk driving). The result of this impairment caused by distraction is that drivers are twenty-three times more likely to have an accident when texting and four times more likely to be involved in a crash if they are talking on a cell phone.

Teens and Distracted Driving

Although adult, experienced drivers are often guilty of distracted driving, most experts believe that young and teenaged drivers are at particular risk for accidents and near-accidents due to distractions. Distraction.gov reports, "Our youngest and most inexperienced drivers are most at risk, with 16% of all distracted driving crashes involving drivers under 20."[14] The Virginia Tech Transportation Institute explains that people between the ages of fifteen and twenty are only 6.4 percent of drivers on the road, but they represent 11.4 percent of accident fatalities and 14 percent of all accidents that cause injuries. Traffic accidents are the leading cause of death in people under the age of thirty-five. Many experts believe that teens are most at risk from distracted driving simply because they are new to driving and are inexperienced.

In 2014, Charlie Klauer and her Virginia Tech research team published the results of a study that examined distracted driving behavior in young, novice drivers. The team conducted a long-term study of two different groups of drivers. The first group consisted of one hundred experienced drivers between the ages of eighteen and seventy-two. Each driver's car was equipped with multiple video cameras and sensors that recorded everything that happened in the vehicle for one year. The second group was made up of forty-two teens who had had their driver's licenses for three or fewer weeks. With the same video cameras and sensors, these teens and their driving were tracked for eighteen months. After the studies were completed, the team collected and analyzed all the data from each vehicle, paying particular attention to instances of "secondary tasks," which is Klauer's term for distractions that may increase the risk of an accident or near-accident.

Charlie Klauer, a researcher at the Virginia Tech Transportation Institute, adjusts a data acquisition system in a vehicle in 2006. Her research has found that distracted driving caused the vast majority of accidents.

The research team found many incidents of performing secondary tasks in both groups of drivers. They dialed and talked on phones, texted, ate, talked to passengers in the car, reached away from the steering wheel, and looked outside windows instead of straight ahead. The novice teen drivers, however, changed their behaviors over time. In the first six months of driving, these teens were cautious while driving. They engaged in secondary tasks much less frequently than did the experienced drivers. By the seventh through the fifteenth months of

Alcohol- and Drug-Impaired Driving

Nearly one-third of fatal crashes in the United States involve an alcohol-impaired driver. In 2012, that meant more than ten thousand people died in alcohol-related crashes. That equals one death every fifty-one minutes. Drugs other than alcohol accounted for 18 percent of fatal vehicle deaths. Although texting while driving is six times more dangerous than driving while intoxicated, driving under the influence continues to be the leading cause of fatalities on the roadways. Fatalities involving drugs and alcohol have decreased among teens over the last few years, according to the National Highway Traffic Safety Administration. More than 90 percent of teens say that they never drink and

Intoxicated drivers cause the majority of accident fatalities.

drive. However, teen deaths in crashes have remained unchanged because distracted driving has increased over the same amount of time.

driving, however, the teens performed secondary tasks as often as the experienced drivers. In the last months of the study, months sixteen through eighteen, novice drivers engaged in secondary tasks twice as often as the older drivers. Klauer explains, "Novice drivers are more likely to engage in high-risk secondary tasks more frequently over time as they became more comfortable with driving. The increasingly high rates of secondary task engagement among newly licensed novice drivers in our study are worrisome as this appears to be an important contributing factor to crashes or near-crashes."[15]

Klauer and her team analyzed whether secondary tasks increased the risk for crashes and near-crashes among both groups of drivers. In the group of experienced drivers, there were 42 crashes and 476 near-crashes during the year of the study. In the much smaller group of novice drivers, there were 31 crashes and 136 near-crashes during the eighteen months they were tracked. Fortunately, none of these events involved deaths or injuries, but many were caused by distracting secondary tasks. The research team concluded that a secondary task had contributed to an accident or near-accident if it occurred within five seconds before the event or within one second after it (because a driver might be so distracted that the accident occurred before he or she became aware of a problem). For experienced drivers, dialing a cell phone seemed to be the only secondary task associated with a crash or near-crash, but the data collected from experienced drivers in this study came from 2003 and 2004, when most adults were not yet engaged in texting, so this distraction was not studied for these drivers. With novice drivers, secondary tasks caused more trouble. The team reports, "Among novice drivers, dialing or reaching for a cell phone, texting, reaching for an object other than a cell phone, looking at a roadside object such as a vehicle in a previous crash, and eating were all associated with a significantly increased risk of a crash or near-crash."[16]

Too Great a Risk

Charlie Klauer and her team conclude that distractions are particularly dangerous for novice drivers, especially when the secondary task requires that they take their eyes away from the road. Klauer sums up, "Newly licensed novice drivers are of course at a particularly high crash risk, in part because driving is a complicated task and novices tend to make more mistakes when learning a new task. In previous studies we found that crash or near-crash rates among the novice drivers were nearly four times higher than for experienced drivers. Therefore, it should not be surprising that secondary task engagement contributes to this heightened risk among novice drivers."[17]

Klauer's research about teen drivers is but one study among many about distracted driving and the dangers it poses for all drivers. The research does not always yield exactly the same results, but overwhelmingly one fact is clear: Distracted driving is dangerous behavior that puts everyone at risk of injury and death.

Texting: The Scariest Distraction

On April 3, 2013, twenty-two-year-old Alex Heit died because of texting and driving. Alex, a student at the University of Northern Colorado, was driving that evening eastbound on a two-lane road just outside the town of Greeley, where his school is located. Alex's car began to drift into the opposite lane, and witnesses later told police that he seemed to have his head down. An oncoming westbound driver slowed his car at the sight of Alex coming toward him and began to veer over. At that moment, Alex looked up, apparently saw the danger, and jerked the steering wheel hard to get back into his lane. Alex overcorrected and lost control of the car. The vehicle left the road and rolled and flipped in the dirt shoulder of the road. Alex was rushed to a nearby hospital, but he died of his injuries shortly after the crash. In the subsequent investigation, police determined that Alex was in the middle of texting with a friend on his iPhone at the time of the accident. Still on the phone was Alex's last text—unfinished and never sent.

Alex's grieving parents, Steve and Sharon Heit, released to the public a photo of his phone showing the messages that had cost their son his life. The last, unfinished message read "Sounds good my man, seeya soon, ill tw." The message was just part of an ordinary, inconsequential, lighthearted conversation that would be Alex's final communication, and his parents wanted others to see it in the hope that no one else would die over a text message. Along with the photo of Alex's phone, his parents released a statement saying, "Please vow to never, NEVER text and drive. In a split second you could ruin your future, injure or kill others and tear a hole in the heart of everyone who loves you." The Greeley police who investigated Alex's fatal crash were also horrified by the cause of his death. He had not been speeding; he was just texting. Police sergeant Susan West added, "That's why the family and the police department want to get the message out there that this can happen to anyone, anytime. If anything good can come from the loss of their son, they want that to be the message—don't text and drive."[18]

Why Do People Text and Drive?

According to the U.S. Department of Transportation, the vast majority of people know that texting and driving is dangerous. In a 2012 national survey by the Department of Transportation, 86 percent of respondents said that driving while sending an e-mail or text was unsafe, and 85 percent said that reading an e-mail or text while driving is unsafe. In a 2012 AT&T Teen Driver Survey, 97 percent of teens aged fifteen through ninteen said that texting and driving is unsafe. Yet, according to the survey,

People use cell phones while driving in Toronto, Ontario, in 2013. Texting while driving is the most dangerous form of distraction.

43 percent of teens text while driving anyway, and almost half of adults admit to doing the same thing. According to Distraction .gov, about 25 percent of teens admit to texting every time they drive. In addition, about 20 percent of teens and 10 percent of their parents report having extended conversations, involving multiple messages, when they are behind the wheel.

Why do so many people text and drive, even though they know it is dangerous? Distraction.gov says, "They make the mistake of thinking the statistics don't apply to them, that they can defy the odds. Still others simply lead busy, stressful lives and use cell phones and smartphones to stay connected with their families, friends, and workplaces. They forget or choose not to shut these devices off when they get behind the wheel."[19] Reporter Sonari Glinton, who works for NPR, says that he is ashamed to admit it, but he is one of the people who knows he should not text and drive but has done it anyway. While he was on the road covering the 2012 presidential election, he says he put in long hours driving the roads in Iowa, Ohio, and Indiana. Several times during that period, he was driving on rural roads, without much traffic, and checked his e-mail, telling himself that it was safe.

Emily Reynolds lost her older sister Cady to texting and driving in 2007, when Cady was just sixteen years old. Cady's car was hit by another sixteen-year-old, who was driving distracted, ran a red light, and hit Cady's car in the intersection. That driver did not even notice that the light was red because she was looking down at her electronic device. She sped through the intersection at 45 to 50 miles per hour (72 to 80kph), never trying to apply the brakes because she never saw the danger. Today, Emily is an ardent spokesperson for safe driving, and she speaks out against texting and driving for the U.S. Department of Transportation. Nevertheless, she also tries to understand why people choose to indulge in such a risky behavior. She once explained during an interview for *Teen Vogue* magazine, "We haven't learned to live without phones, so we think that when we start driving, we can use them in the car and be fine."[20]

Not Everyone Gets It

When Australian driver Kimberley Davis ran into a bicyclist in 2013, she was not apologetic but angry. Davis did not believe that distracted driving had caused the accident. The cyclist suffered serious injuries, including a spinal fracture and a lacerated head and body. Davis, however, was distressed over the dents in her expensive car from the bicycle. She said, "I don't agree that people texting and driving could hit a cyclist. I wasn't on my phone when I hit the cyclist." A police check of her phone records suggested otherwise. While driving that day, she had used her phone 44 times and sent and received 22 text messages. The last message was just 51 seconds before she made a call for emergency help after the accident. Two days after the crash, when asked about the crash and her phone use, she answered, "I just don't care." In court, Davis pleaded guilty to "dangerous driving," was fined $4,500, and had her license suspended for nine months.

Quoted in Andrew Thomson. "'I Just Don't Care': Texting P-plate Driver Hits Cyclist." *The Standard,* April 15, 2014. www.standard.net.au/story/2219242/i-just-dont-care-texting-p-plate-driver-hits-cyclist.

The Habit of Texting

Scott W. Campbell, a professor of telecommunications at the University of Michigan, agrees with Emily that the use of cell phones, smartphones, and mobile communication in general has become habitual for most people in America. He thinks that activities such as texting have become such strong habits for most people that they use electronic devices without even thinking about it—"like a reflex." Campbell explains:

> My colleague Rich Ling is a sociologist who argues that the "new thing" about mobile communication today is that it's "nothing new." What he means is that mobile communication has become so deeply embedded in our social structure that it is now a taken-for-granted social fact. Of course the technology and interface will continue to change and offer new things. But mobile communication as a practice has become rooted into the very foundation of social life. It is no longer something that is nice

to have; it is now a basic expectation. It is no longer just your problem if you do not have a mobile phone—it is a problem for others as well. Ling's argument is that, over time, expectations for accessibility have become universally heightened as a result of having virtually anytime-anywhere access to each other, not to mention information and other forms of content. The idea is that mobile communication, as something we (pretty much) all commonly do, has transformed from new and revolutionary into a taken-for-granted part of everyday life, much like clocks and automotive transportation.[21]

Excuses People Tell Themselves

Perhaps people are so dependent on their phones that they habitually feel that they must read or answer text messages while they drive. However, many people come up with rationalizations for texting and driving. At the website Don't Text & Drive, some of the justifications given include:

- Reading a text is safer than composing and sending one.
- They hold the phone near the windshield "for better visibility."
- They increase following distance.
- They text only at a stop sign or red light.[22]

Because of justifications like these, 77 percent of young adult drivers believe that they can safely text while driving, and 55 percent of them say that texting while driving is easy. In part, people think they can text safely because they have engaged in the behavior and not experienced any problems. Daniel V. McGehee, a professor and researcher at the University of Iowa, has been studying vehicle accidents for more than twenty years. When he talks about the dangers of texting and driving, he means any interactive smartphone behaviors, such as texting, e-mailing, Snapchatting, or using Twitter, Instagram, or Facebook. McGehee explains that people often do not recognize the risk. He says, "Most of the time we get away with distraction, which encourages us to push it a little more, and a little more. Sure we may drift out of our lane on occasion, or have to slam on the brakes when we don't see the car stopped ahead. But the fact is the roadway environment is largely a forgiving one."[23] It is only when an emergency or an unexpected event occurs that the danger becomes clear—often too late for the texting driver to avoid.

When Nicole Meredith was seventeen years old, she almost did not get away with her distracted behavior. The Kentucky teen was driving to a friend's house when she decided to text the friend to tell her that she would be at her house in about five minutes. Nicole hit send and then looked up through the windshield. Already the front end of her car was on the grass that divided the freeway. She had no control of the car as it spun and then hit

A teen looks at a text message while driving. Some people mistakenly believe that reading a text is safer than writing one.

three different barriers in the median that blocked her from sailing across into oncoming traffic. The car came to a stop in the median. Nicole was not hurt, but the car was completely destroyed, and the teen was terrified. She knew the accident had been her fault and did not admit to her parents for months that she had been texting. When she finally admitted the cause of the crash to her parents, her father said that she had cheated death that day. Nicole knows that is true. Looking back, she cannot imagine why she felt the need to text her friend when she would see her in five minutes anyway. Nicole says, "I could have just waited." At the time, she explains, "To me, texting was just a second nature. I really didn't think that it was something that was bad to do."[24]

Dangerous Distractions from Multiple Sources

Almost everyone who texts and drives makes the decision because he or she thinks that this time it will be safe to do or because he or she is a good enough driver to get away with it. David Strickland of the National Highway Traffic Safety Administration says, "Many drivers see distracted driving as risky when other drivers do it, but do not recognize how their own driving deteriorates."[25] No one can text or read a text without being distracted. This fact has been proven many times with many different scientific studies. Also, texting is the most dangerous distraction because it involves all three types of distractions. Whether reading or sending a text, the driver must look at the phone, handle the phone, and devote a portion of his or her mind to the phone.

NO TEXT MATTERS THAT MUCH

"There is nothing that important that they should put their life or anybody else's life in jeopardy over a text."—Anthony Arminio, injured victim of a texting driver

Quoted in David Chang. "Driver, Victim Speak on Dangers of Texting While Driving." NBC10.com, February 27, 2014. www.nbcphiladelphia.com/news/local/Driver-Victim -Speak-on-Dangers-of-Texting-While-Driving-247427021.html.

Texting is much more distracting than most people realize.

Visually, texting is surprisingly distracting. According to Distraction.gov, the minimum amount of time a texting driver's eyes are off the road is 4.6 seconds. When a car is going 55 miles per hour (88.5kph), almost 5 seconds is enough time to travel the length of a football field without looking. During that time, the situation is as if the car were driving itself since the driver is not aware of the road, his or her own car, or other drivers and pedestrians. Some drivers think that they are glancing back and forth between the phone and the road as they are texting, but that is not true. These people still average about 4.6 seconds with their eyes not on the road. This serious visual distraction is a large part of the reason that people who text and drive are twenty-three times more likely to be involved in a crash than drivers who do not text. Even at a stop sign or red light, explains Daniel McGehee, texting or e-mailing is dangerous. He says, "Some of the most intense distractions can come when you're stopped."[26] Texting means that the driver is unaware of pedestrians and other cars at intersections, and the driver's brain and eyes needs time to shift from texting to driving. In these situations, rear-end collisions are common for people who text.

Manually, texting requires reaching for the phone, holding the phone, and typing a message, and that means releasing one's hold on the steering wheel. With the goal of eliminating this distraction and some visual distraction as well, automakers are incorporating hands-free technology into vehicles, so that people can text and e-mail using voice commands. Hands-free text messaging systems read incoming texts out loud on command. Some then offer the option of tapping the touch screen just once in order to send one of fifteen preset replies, including the reply that the driver is busy and cannot reply at that moment. Other systems allow the driver to use voice-to-text technology to speak their own texts, have them translated to written texts, and then send the messages. Automobile manufacturers believe these hands-free technologies make texting and driving safer, but so far, scientific studies find quite the opposite effect: People actually concentrate more when using voice-to-text or even listening to incoming texts than they do when they are manually texting. They are more visually and cognitively distracted by hands-free technology than they are by texting on their phones.

At the University of Utah, researcher David Strayer conducted one study of voice-activated messaging systems. He and his team measured eye movements, brain waves, head movements, and driving behaviors in thirty-two college students as they drove. The researchers also measured the drivers' reaction time—how fast the drivers could react to an event, such as a light turning red or a need to quickly apply the brakes. The students and their reactions were studied as they performed several

Disabled for Life

One night in August 2011, fifty-two-year-old Deborah Drewniak was walking her dog along the side of the road when she was struck by a car driven by eighteen-year-old Emma Vieira. About forty-five seconds before the crash, Vieira had left her house, and police said that in that time period, she had received four text messages and sent one. Vieira admitted that she was distracted and just had not seen Drewniak. Vieira felt terrible about having hit Drewniak, but her regret could not change Drewniak's severe injuries. Almost every bone in Drewniak's body was broken, and she is permanently brain damaged. She says she has lost her independence and must depend on others to live the rest of her life. She cannot speak clearly and needs help with most daily activities. Nevertheless, Drewniak is determined to spread the word about the horrors of texting and driving. With a friend to translate for her, she speaks to high school students about preventing such tragedies. In one presentation, she declared, "Using a cell phone while driving was deliberate and intentional. She hit me deliberately and intentionally. Don't use your cell phone while you're driving. Shut your cell phone off."

Deborah Drewniak sustained permanent injuries after being hit by a teenager who was texting and driving.

Quoted in Logan Crawford. "Victim Warns Vt. Teens About Dangers of Texting While Driving." WCAX .com, May 12, 2014. www.wcax.com/story/25475238 /victim-warns-vt-teens-about-dangers-of-texting -while-driving.

distracting activities. Of all the distractions, speech-to-text was the worst, as measured by driver performance. Strayer and his team explain that drivers were concentrating on the technology so intently that they developed "tunnel vision." Their eyes stopped scanning the road, and they tended to stare straight ahead. In addition, the drivers had to think carefully about speaking clearly and precisely so that the computer-driven system would accurately text their messages. Other studies have found that even listening to an incoming text was distracting because the computer voice is artificial and can be hard to understand. Also, drivers have been shown to be visually distracted by voice-to-text technology because they look to be sure that the message was typed correctly by the computer. Strayer says, "Our research shows that hands-free is not risk-free. These new, speech-based technologies in the car can overload the driver's attention and impair their ability to drive safely. An unintended consequence of trying to make driving safer—by moving to speech-to-text, in-vehicle systems—may actually overload the driver and make them less safe."[27]

Multitasking Is a Myth

The cognitive distraction of texting and driving appears to be very intense, whether the texting is manual or voice-activated. When drivers concentrate on reading or writing a text, they cannot concentrate on driving. The reason lies in the way the brain works. Contrary to what many people believe, the brain cannot think about two things at the same time. It cannot multitask. Earl K. Miller is a neuroscientist at the Massachusetts Institute of Technology who has studied the brain and multitasking for many years. He explains, "People can't multitask very well, and when people say they can, they're deluding themselves. The brain is very good at deluding itself. Switching from task to task, you think you're actually paying attention to everything around you at the same time. But you're actually not. You're not paying attention to one or two things simultaneously, but switching between them very rapidly."[28] That switching takes time, even if only fractions of a second, and the time adds up to significant periods of inattention for a texting driver. Also, Miller says, the brain can handle only a finite amount of information. Each time it must cognitively switch between tasks, it experiences a small stumble, a bit of confusion that diminishes its efficiency and focus. The more tasks that the brain has to handle, the less able it is to process information smoothly and the more inattentive to detail it becomes.

IT'S THE OTHER GUY

"There's a belief out there that everybody is the problem except me, when actually you, in fact, are the problem. There's a belief that if you're on the road traveling, one little text won't hurt that much. But when you have 30 million people out on the road and each of them wants to send just one little text, that's when (crashes) happen."—Sarah Gavin, Expedia travel expert

Quoted in Larry Copeland. "Grrr! Texting While Driving Really Annoys Other Motorists." *USA Today*, May 16, 2014. www.usatoday.com/story/news/nation/2014/05/16/texting-drivers-are-annoying/9135209.

In many studies in his Applied Cognition Laboratory, David Strayer has also determined that human brains cannot handle more than one task at a time. In one 2013 study, Strayer and his research team evaluated the ability of 310 college students to multitask while driving. The team also asked the students whether they were good at multitasking in order to determine if people could judge their skills. Surprisingly, Strayer and his team discovered that drivers who called themselves good multitaskers were usually the worst at it. The team concluded that drivers who multitask do so most often because they are not good at focusing on a single job (driving). They are easily distracted people. Strayer says, "If you have people who are multitasking a lot, you might come to the conclusion they are good at multitasking. In fact, the more likely they are to do it, the more likely they are to be bad at it."[29]

Real People, Real Results

Extensive research and scientific investigation clearly demonstrate why it is frighteningly risky to text and drive, and many

In New York State, which has one of the toughest no-texting-while-driving laws in the United States, a highway sign encourages drivers to stop at a rest area to text.

real-world personal tragedies testify to the truth of the science. Charlene Lake, a vice president for AT&T, which is committed to spreading the word of the dangers of texting and driving, says that just an instant of inattention while driving can change someone's life forever. She explains that statistics are impressive enough, but that the story of a young man named Wil Craig impacted her as no statistics ever had. Lake met Craig and heard his story at a conference about texting and driving in 2012. In

2008, seventeen-year-old Craig was on the way to the movies with his girlfriend. The girlfriend was the one driving and Craig was her front seat passenger. Craig's girlfriend was speeding and, at the same time, she looked down at her phone to read an incoming text. When she looked up and saw that she was veering off the road, she tried to brake, missed the pedal, and hit the accelerator instead. The car sped up and crashed into a tree at the side of the road. Although his girlfriend was unhurt, Craig suffered severe injuries, including a collapsed lung, four broken ribs, and severe brain trauma. Firefighters cut Craig from the car and rushed him to the hospital, where he spent eight weeks in a coma. Doctors gave him only a 4 percent chance of survival, and when Craig defied the odds and lived, they predicted that he would never walk or talk again. After extensive rehabilitation therapy and with great courage and strength of will, Craig did overcome his injuries. He walks and talks differently than he once did, but he was able to graduate from high school and move on to college. Still, says Craig, "It's a battle everyday just to get up and look at myself in the mirror."[30]

Today, Craig shares the story of what happened to him to encourage others never to text while driving. His story so touched Charlene Lake that she wants everyone to know about it. She says, "Part of my job at AT&T is to help lead our company's efforts to put an end to texting while driving. And the statistics I see every day are terrifying. But here's the problem with statistics: After a while, they become background noise. It's easy to lose sight of the real people behind these numbers. I want you to remember Wil. As he will be the first to tell you, no text or email is worth risking your life."[31]

DANGEROUS PHONE CONVERSATIONS

Many people believe that just talking on a phone while driving is safe, especially if they do so using hands-free headsets, but both science and driver experiences indicate otherwise. Phone conversations while driving are dangerous cognitive distractions that increase the chance of accidents fourfold. Just reaching for or dialing a phone triples the chance of an accident. Talking on a phone is not the same as talking with passengers. Phone conversations may include the added manual distractions of reaching for, dialing, and holding the phone, and also include different attentional demands than when talking to a passenger.

Distracted Manually and Visually

Just the split-second manual and visual distraction of reaching for a cell phone at the wrong moment can cause a car accident. In 2014, for example, in North Vancouver, Canada, a thirty-five-year-old male driver was distracted from the roadway when he reached down for his cell phone, which had fallen onto the center console of his vehicle. In that moment, the man's inattention caused him to veer toward the right side of the road and he crash into a parked car. A chain reaction ensued, in which three other vehicles crashed as they tried to avoid the incident. Fortunately, no one was injured in the crash, but the financial loss was substantial. Police sergeant Dave Drewers, who responded to the accident, says that it could have been much worse. He explains, "The consequences could have been much more serious if the driver had swerved left on the busy roadway. This is another striking reminder not to engage with your cell phone while driving."[32]

In California in 2012, a ringing cell phone caused a much more terrible accident. A driver reached for his ringing cell phone and dropped it on the floor. He reached down to pick it up, veered out of his lane into oncoming traffic, and hit another car head on. The driver and all three of his passengers were injured and hospitalized. The driver of the car he hit, an eighty-eight-year-old man, was killed, and the eighty-four-year-old female passenger was seriously injured. Writer Kiernan Hopkins comments on the case, "Just another example of how dangerous it is to drive distractedly, eyes off the road for just a second, can cause injuries or death."[33]

Talking on hands-free cell phones has been shown to be as distracting as talking on a handheld device.

Cognitively Distracted

Talking on a cell phone can be as dangerous as reaching for one. In Maryland in 2011, Susan Yum lost her five-year-old son because of a phone conversation. Yum, her husband James Owen, and their two children were sitting in their car, stopped in backed-up traffic from a previous accident. As they sat in the traffic jam, an SUV slammed into the back of their car at a speed of 62 miles per hour (99.8kph). Devin McKeiver, the driver of the SUV, was talking on his cell phone and did not even notice that the traffic ahead of him on the roadway was stopped. He never had time to apply his brakes. Yum's husband's shoulder was shattered in the crash, but he leapt from the car and yelled for   door, turned
arc   crying in pain.
Al   onscious, with
bl

ed by a cell
off the brake
"—Canadian
l Louis Hugo

ancescutti. "Fatal
ian vol. 59, no. 7

nd then rescue
pe   continues the
story,

> At the hospital, I walked by a gurney with a pool of blood on the bottom and I wondered if it's my son's. Hospital officials came to get me after Alex was whisked away by a team of doctors and nurses. They told me it didn't look

Blind to the Gorilla

In 1999, psychologists Daniel Simons and Christopher Chabris conducted a now-famous experiment about inattention blindness. They asked a group of subjects to watch a short video of six people playing basketball. Three wore white shirts and three wore black shirts. The subjects were told to count the number of passes of the ball made by the white-shirted players. During the video of the game, a gorilla (actually a woman in a gorilla suit) walks into the middle of the players, turns to the camera, and thumps its chest. After nine seconds, the gorilla walks away. Simons and Chabris ask today, "Would you see the gorilla? Almost everyone has the intuition that the answer is 'yes, of course I would.' How could something so obvious go completely unnoticed? But when we did this experiment at Harvard University several years ago, we found that half of the people who watched the video and counted the passes missed the gorilla. It was as though the gorilla was invisible." They explain, "This experiment reveals two things: that we are missing a lot of what goes on around us, and that we have no idea that we are missing so much."

Christopher Chabris and Daniel Simons. "The Invisible Gorilla." www.theinvisiblegorilla.com/gorilla_experiment.html.

good and that I should go to the trauma room where [Jake] was. I was so terrified that I was tempted to refuse to go with them, and then when I realized that if he was going to die, I could not let my son die among only strangers. When I entered the room, I noticed that Jake's feet were bare and all I could focus on were his little toes, and doctors were working on him so furiously. Then one of the doctors said the dreaded words that no mother wants to hear. He said, "Mom, we have to call it."[34]

Jake was dead.

McKeiver was eventually charged in the accident and found guilty in court of negligent driving and failing to control his speed. He admitted that he had been distracted and talking on his phone at the time of the accident, and he knows that he has to bear the guilt for Jake's death for the rest of his life. McKeiver's defense attorney said after the court case was over, "He just broke down in tears. They were not tears of joy [because he was not sentenced to prison]; they were tears of sadness for the Owen family. He understands he was negligent and wrong."[35]

Phone Talking and Driver Errors

Cell phone conversations while driving may be more dangerous than texting, not because talking is more distracting, but because it is so much more common. According to the National Safety Council, the use of cell phones is the number-one most common cause of distracted driving, and more than 66 percent of drivers admit to talking on their phones while driving. At any moment during the day, at least 9 percent of drivers are talking on a cell phone. In many ways, say researchers, all these cell phone conversations make people poorer drivers than if they drove with their undivided attention on the road.

In one observational study at the University of Utah, David Strayer and his team sat at a four-way intersection in Salt Lake City over a period of four days and watched 1,748 drivers as they came up to the stop signs to see if each driver really came to a full stop. The researchers could see the drivers and note whether they were using a cell phone. They recorded cell phone use for every driver and whether each of the drivers came to a full stop. The results of this study were dramatic. Three out of every four drivers using a phone did not come to a complete stop (or any stop) at the stop signs. But when drivers were not using a phone, only one out of every five failed to stop. The researchers conclude that the chance of committing a traffic violation while conversing on a cell phone is ten times greater than the chance for a nondistracted driver.

Stop signs are not the only visual cues missed by drivers talking on cell phones. According to the National Safety Council, drivers using cell phones often also fail to see red lights and highway exit signs. In addition, they are more likely to drift out of their own lane and to have slower reaction times in braking, accelerating, or turning the steering wheel. In summary, says

Talking on the phone is the most common cause of distracted driving.

the National Safety Council's website, "Drivers talking on cell phones miss half of the information in their driving environment."[36] The cause of this failure to notice environmental information is cognitive distraction, and it occurs whether a driver is using a phone manually or hands-free. It is inattention blindness, not the distraction of looking at the phone.

Inattention Blindness

Inattention blindness, explains psychologist Arien Mack, is "looking without seeing." It is "the failure to see highly visible objects we may be looking at directly when our attention is elsewhere." Mack adds, "This is why talking on cell telephones while driving is a distinctly bad idea."[37] Inattention blindness is a brain problem, not a visual problem, and it affects everyone's brain.

In 2007, David Strayer and his colleague Frank A. Drews reported on their studies of inattention blindness, which used a computerized driving simulator in their laboratory. The simulator consisted of a driver's seat, dashboard, steering wheel, and brake and gas pedals that exactly mimic a Ford Crown Victoria sedan with automatic transmission. Through the windshield, each of the subjects in their studies looked at a high-resolution display of a roadway with realistic driving scenes, including traffic signs and signals, pedestrians, other cars, and buildings. The simulator provided a 180-degree view, just as does the windshield of a real vehicle. When a test subject was driving in the simulator, cameras and computers recorded eye movements and reaction times, such as how long it took a subject to hit the brakes.

In one of Strayer and Drews's studies, subjects first drove through a simulated road course with thirty different objects added to the computerized display. Objects included such things

Pedestrians should be vigilant about watching for distracted drivers when crossing busy urban streets.

as billboards, other cars, trucks, pedestrians, a child playing on the edge of the road, and traffic signs. Half of the test subjects in the driving simulator performed normal driving tasks with full attention on the roadway. The other half were required to carry on a phone conversation using a hands-free system. After the driving simulation, all the subjects of the experiment were asked to identify what objects they remembered seeing as they drove along the roadway. The researchers were able to compare the objects remembered to whether the subject's eyes had stared at the object. No matter what the object and no matter how long the subject had stared at the object, drivers talking on phones remembered far fewer objects than drivers who were not distracted. Unlike the nondistracted drivers, the test subjects engaged in phone conversations missed half of the objects and information presented in the driving environment. Strayer and Drews conclude, "Even when cellphone drivers direct their gaze at objects in the driving environment, they often fail to 'see' them because attention has been diverted to the cellphone conversation."[38]

It's the Phone, Stupid!

In another study with the driving simulator, the researchers asked half of their subjects to engage in a hands-free cell phone conversation and the other half to converse with a front seat passenger. The researchers wanted to know if phone conversations were more distracting than just talking to someone in the car. In this experiment, all the drivers were told to drive about 8 miles (12k) down a freeway and then exit the freeway at a rest stop. About 88 percent of the drivers talking to a passenger completed the task successfully, but only 50 percent of those on cell phones were able to do so. Part of the reason that passengers were less distracting than cell phones was that the passengers often reminded the drivers to turn off at the correct exit, which, of course, the cell phone conversationalist could not do. Strayer and Drews say that the give-and-take of a phone conversation interferes with the ability to process information in the driving environment.

Experiments have shown that distractions from passengers are less dangerous than distractions caused by cell phones.

In another study with the driving simulator, subjects were asked to follow a pace car in front of them that was programmed to apply its brakes periodically. The researchers collected data on the reaction time of each driver—how long it took each one to apply the brakes in response to the slowing car ahead. A driver's failure to notice the pace car's brake lights and changed speed at all resulted in his or her "crashing" into the rear end of the pace car, just like in real-world traffic situations. If the driver did apply his or her brakes successfully, the pace car sped up again, and the researchers also measured how quickly each subject responded to that acceleration by stepping on the gas pedal again. Some of the drivers in this study were nondistracted, while some talked on handheld cell phones and some used hands-free phones. In all instances, compared to the nondistracted drivers, those on cell phones had slower reaction times. They took longer to brake in response to the pace car and were slower to accelerate once the pace car sped up again. Whether the drivers were on handheld or hands-free phones made no difference. Drivers having cell phone conversations took longer to notice red brake lights and to apply their own brakes. Even though they were staring directly at the pace car ahead of them, they suffered with inattention blindness, at least temporarily. Some even were involved in simulated accidents as they rear-ended the pace car. They looked but did not see.

Looking and Not Seeing

Inattention blindness was the cause of twelve-year-old Joe Teater's death in 2004. Joe's mother, Judy, explains,

> On Jan. 19, 2004, Joe and I were on our way to an after school activity. We were driving down an urban divided highway when a 20-year-old woman, driving a Hummer while talking on her cell phone, ran a red light and slammed in the passenger side of my car, killing Joe. The driver of the Hummer passed four cars and a school bus that had all stopped at the red light. She never applied her brakes, and witnesses reported seeing her talking on her cell phone and looking straight out the front window. She was looking, but she didn't see the red light or realize that she should have stopped. She didn't see the three cars before me cross the intersection, but she was looking straight ahead. This is what we mean when we say drivers suffer cognitive distraction. Their minds are distracted, and they aren't paying attention.[39]

Inattention blindness is not a problem with vision and is not caused by a driver not caring about paying attention. It is a function of the way the human brain processes information and its inability to multitask. David Strayer says that inattention blindness is the result of a kind of bottleneck that occurs in the brain as it tries to switch between tasks. It affects everyone. In order to understand the distraction of cell phone conversations, scientists look to how the brain works.

Dave Teater holds a photo of his twelve-year-old son, Joseph, who was killed by a distracted driver.

What Happens in the Brain

Everything that people perceive, whether through sight, hearing, feeling, smelling, or tasting, is called sensory information. All of the sensory information perceived in the environment must be committed to short-term memory by the brain before it can be consciously recognized, acted on, or transferred to long-term memory. This is also true for everything people think. The brain can hold perceptions or thoughts in short-term memory for a few seconds, but in order to get any information into short-term memory for this few seconds, the brain must go through a process in which it prioritizes and processes the information. Scientists categorize this process into six distinct stages. In the first stage, the brain has to "select" which bit of all sensory information in the environment to pay attention to. The selection may be conscious or unconscious, but it is necessary because the environment offers so many pieces of sensory information that

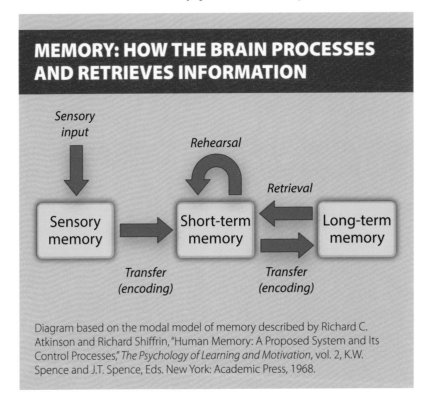

MEMORY: HOW THE BRAIN PROCESSES AND RETRIEVES INFORMATION

Diagram based on the modal model of memory described by Richard C. Atkinson and Richard Shiffrin, "Human Memory: A Proposed System and Its Control Processes," *The Psychology of Learning and Motivation*, vol. 2, K.W. Spence and J.T. Spence, Eds. New York: Academic Press, 1968.

the brain cannot pay attention to them all. Brain attention capacity is finite; that is, the brain has a limited capacity for attention. A driver's brain, for example, may select the sight of a stoplight or the sound of an ambulance siren for attention while screening out a telephone wire on the side of the road or the chirp of a bird in a tree. Once the selection is made, the brain must next "process" the piece of sensory information. It must accurately determine what the sensory information is. It decides, "That is a siren" or "That is a stoplight." Then, the brain must "encode" the information and make a memory, and then "store" that information in short-term memory. Encoding is the process by which the brain makes a mental representation or image of the sensory information. Storage allows the brain to hold the information, at least for a few seconds.

INFORMATION NOT PROCESSED

"There is a standard code for crash investigations called roughly 'look, but didn't see.' In other words, I was looking in the right place, but I didn't register what was there."—Jim Hedlund, safety consultant

Quoted in Daily Mail Reporter. "Even Hands-Free Phones Are Dangerous While Driving, New Research Reveals." Mail Online, December 15, 2011. www.dailymail.co.uk/news /article-2074661/Even-hands-free-phones-dangerous-driving-new-research-reveals .html.

At this point in the brain's activity, different areas of the brain may become engaged. Sometimes, the information is transferred to long-term memory. Other times, it remains in short-term memory. To act upon the stored memory, the brain must go through the final two stages. It must "retrieve" the memory, and lastly "execute," which means to act on the information. In this last stage of the process, a driver may, for instance, consciously recognize the siren sound as from an ambulance and pull over to let the emergency vehicle go by. Generally, the brain performs all of the stages of processing sensory information so

Driving on the Back Burner

The National Safety Council (NSC) compares talking on a phone while driving to cooking on the stove with pots on all the burners. Suppose the cook is stirring one pot, when suddenly another pot starts to boil over. The person must quickly shift tasks by grabbing a potholder and removing the lid from the boiling pot, while being careful not to get burned by escaping steam. What happens to the first pot? If the cook tries to keep stirring with one hand, chances are that he or she will not be able to keep the motion going smoothly. The spoon will move jerkily or not at all. If the boiling-over pot demands too much attention, the cook will have to put the spoon down, ignore the first pot, and tend to the primary problem first. If a cook cannot give equal attention to two pots on a stovetop, how much harder it must be to attend to two much more complex tasks—driving and carrying on a phone conversation. Both tasks cannot have the driver's primary attention. NSC asks, "Should driving a vehicle ever be a 'back burner' task?"

National Safety Council. "Understanding the Distracted Brain." White paper, March 2010, p. 7. www .nsc.org/safety_road/Distracted_Driving/Documents /Dstrct_Drvng_White_Paper_1_2011.pdf.

quickly and smoothly that people respond to their environment almost automatically and with a high level of efficiency. However, because the brain's capacity for attention is limited, people who try to multitask can find themselves in trouble. Their brains are overloaded with too much information coming in for them to handle it all. Inattention blindness may occur because the brain is shifting back and forth in its selecting, processing, and encoding. It fails to focus on some important information and filters out information that it should have encoded. No memory is formed, not even short-term memory, and so no conscious awareness that an action should be taken ever occurs. The National Safety Council explains:

> When people attempt to perform two cognitively complex tasks such as driving and talking on a phone, the brain shifts its focus (people develop 'inattention blind-

ness'). . . . Important information falls out of view and is not processed by the brain. For example, drivers may not see a red light. Because this is a process people are not aware of, it's virtually impossible for people to realize they are mentally taking on too much.[40]

In the practical sense, this failure of the brain to process information means that when someone says, "I didn't see the light was red," he or she is not lying. The statement is absolutely true.

Pictures of Distracted Brains

Using a driving simulator and a brain scanning technique known as functional magnetic resonance imaging (fMRI), scientists at Carnegie Mellon University have studied what actually happens in the brain when people try to talk on phones while driving. fMRI is a medical technique for measuring brain activity. It uses a large magnet to create a magnetic field around a person's head. Radio waves are sent through the field, and a computer reads the wave signals and builds a complete picture of the brain. Scientists can get an image of blood flow and changes to blood flow that occur in different areas of the brain in response to activity or perception. As any part of the brain is activated, blood flow increases to that area in response to increased demand on the nerve cells. Scientists can measure the exact amount of this blood flow with fMRI technology and thus determine how well the brain is responding to a demanding activity.

IT MAKES NO SENSE

"Would you ever consider talking on the phone while you're reading a book? . . . So if you'd never consider trying to read a book while talking on the phone, why would you drive while talking on the phone?"—David Teater, director of the National Safety Council

Quoted in Kelly Wallace. "Steering Teen Drivers Out of Harm's Way." CNN, January 23, 2014. www.cnn.com/2014/01/23/living/teens-driving-texting-drinking-parents.

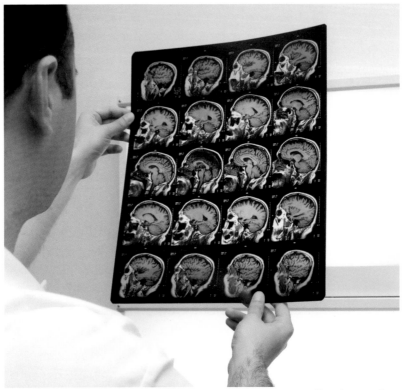

A technician examines a functional magnetic resonance imaging (fMRI) scan of a brain. Researchers have used fMRIs to determine that the brain's parietal lobe is especially important in driving.

With fMRI techniques, it is possible to observe what actual working brains are doing in response to sensory input. The brain is divided into four lobes—the frontal lobe, the parietal lobe, the temporal lobe, and the occipital lobe. Different areas are responsible for different activities. Scientists have determined that the parietal lobe is especially important for the task of driving. It is crucial to navigation and spatial processing as a person drives down a roadway. In their study, Carnegie Mellon's scientists asked their subjects to drive in a simulator while their brain function was measured by the fMRI scanner. In addition, half of the subjects were asked to listen to spoken sentences while driving and say whether the sentences were true or false. This task was assumed to be similar to talking on a phone while driving.

The other half of the subjects were assumed to be driving without the distraction of listening, thinking, and responding.

At the end of the study, the scientists looked at the images of all of their subjects' brains as they drove in the simulator, paying particular attention to the blood flow in their parietal lobes. The results were striking. The brains of the subjects listening to sentences showed 37 percent less blood flow to the parietal lobe than the parietal lobes of subjects who drove without distraction. The scientists also found that listening to sentences decreased blood flow to the occipital lobe where visual input is processed by the brain. The actual driving performance in the simulator demonstrated decreased visual capabilities, too. People listening to sentences often wove out of their lanes or hit guardrails during the study. As do many other scientists, the Carnegie Mellon researchers concluded that human brains do not have the capacity to perform simultaneous tasks without a decrease in performance on both tasks. Phone conversations while driving always impair driving ability.

ALL THE MOMENTARY DISTRACTIONS

Cell phone use while driving gets most of the attention when it comes to distracted driving, because talking and texting are so obviously dangerous. In reality, however, any distracting behaviors can influence driver awareness and driving safety. Visually, manually, and cognitively, anything that takes attention away from the complex task of driving—even briefly—can be a menace on the roadway. It is a matter of failing to focus on the road at the wrong moment.

Teens and Their Distracting Passengers

For teen drivers, one of the most serious nonphone distractions is the presence of passengers or friends in the car. Scientific studies, such as those by David Strayer and Frank Drews, suggest that adult passengers are not very distracting for adult drivers. Adult passengers tend to notice and remark on such events as road hazards, stop signs, and exit signs. They also modulate their conversations when road conditions warrant. For instance, if the driver is trying to navigate a difficult turn or a car darts out in front of the driver's vehicle, the passenger stops talking and waits until the driver has successfully gotten past the situation before resuming the conversation. Thus, adult passengers do not seem to present an important distraction most of the time. With teen drivers and passengers, however, this is not the case. According to a 2012 study by the American Automobile Association (AAA), the risk of a fatal crash for teen drivers increases as the number of teen passengers in the vehicle increases. One teen passenger

Passengers can be distracting, especially for inexperienced teen drivers.

increases the risk of a fatal crash by 44 percent. Having two passengers doubles the risk, and the risk quadruples with three or more young passengers. Interestingly, if a teen driver has at least one passenger in the car who is age thirty-five or older, the risk of a fatal crash decreases by 62 percent.

Scientists are not sure why teens are so at risk when they carry teen passengers in their vehicles. Some evidence suggests that for male teen drivers, teen passengers increase aggressive, risk-taking behaviors, such as speeding or making illegal maneuvers. In one 2011 research study by Allison E. Curry and her research team, the scientists analyzed reports of accidents from the National Motor Vehicle Crash Causation Survey involving 677 teen drivers. Curry's team did find that male teen drivers were encouraged or egged on by male peers to engage in risky driving behaviors. But the other major cause of accidents found in the study was distraction. Passengers were major distractions both for male and female teen drivers. Teen drivers conversed with their passengers, looked at their passengers, and watched their activities and movements. Sometimes, passengers engaged in distracting horseplay. The drivers were more likely to perform distracting activities in the car, too, such as eating, reaching for an object on the floor of the car, or tuning the radio than they did when driving alone. The drivers also looked at external events more when passengers were in the car. They looked at other cars or focused on people on nearby sidewalks. The researchers conclude, "In this study, we found that passengers increase the likelihood of distraction for both male and female teen drivers involved in a crash. Further, our finding that a significant proportion of distracted drivers were reportedly distracted directly by the movements or actions of their passengers makes this issue particularly salient [important]."[41]

Were the Passengers the Cause?

Allison Curry and her team say that much more needs to be learned about how and how often teen passengers distract teen drivers, but determining the cause of an accident is often difficult. In many tragic cases, investigators can see only the fact that a group of teens was involved in yet another terrible crash. In 2013, for example, in rural Texas, sixteen-year-old Jacob Paul Stipe was driving his SUV with four teen friends as his passengers. As he came to an intersection of two country roads, Jacob failed to stop at a stop sign and was hit by a gas tanker truck that had the right of way. Both car and truck burst into flames. All five teens were killed, as was the truck driver. No one knows why Jacob missed the stop sign. Investigators can only speculate that distraction, in a car full of teens, may have been part of the cause of the tragedy.

Josh Douglas, however, knows for certain that distraction was the cause of the near-disaster that threatened him and his teen passengers. In 2014, Josh, a Pennsylvania high school se-

Looking at His Sandwich

In the summer of 2014, a Delaware truck driver was driving on a New Jersey highway while eating a sandwich. The driver, Willard May, took his eyes off the road momentarily to look down at his food. In that brief moment, traffic stopped ahead of him, and when he looked back up, it was too late for him to stop. He crashed into the rear of a car that was then impelled into another lane and crashed into a third car with enough force to push it off the highway and onto the shoulder of the road. One woman was injured, and May was given a ticket for careless driving and following too closely. Even though eating while driving is not legally considered distracted driving in New Jersey, distraction was the cause of the accident.

Eating while driving is not legally considered distracted driving, but eating has been found to be the cause of many accidents.

nior, was driving a group of friends to a bowling alley one afternoon. When a vehicle behind his own car honked at him, Josh and his friends thought they recognized the car of another friend. Josh's passengers started noisily joking around about the friend and waving. Josh looked back at the car, opened his window, took his hand off the wheel to wave, and honked back at the car. For the whole group of friends, it was all in fun. "But," says Josh, "out of nowhere, the car behind me swerved into my lane and cut me off. He was about to sideswipe me. He drove furiously like an animal in the wild about to pounce on its prey. It was not my friend from school—it was an elderly man who made a crude gesture at me." Josh swerved sharply to avoid the aggressive driver, but he was shaken up by the experience. He says that he learned from the near-miss not to let himself be distracted by other cars or by friends inside the car. He says, "I was lucky to avoid getting into an accident."[42]

A Whole List of Distractions

Passengers are but one source of distraction for teens, and, of course, adults as well as teens can be distracted by a myriad of incidents as they are driving down the road. In 2013, the Erie Insurance Company published its analysis of two years' worth of information on fatal crashes compiled by the National Highway Traffic Safety Administration—both for teens and adults. Of the 65,000 deaths recorded, 10 percent, or 6,500, reportedly involved a distraction. The top ten distractions that caused fatal accidents were:

1. Generally distracted or "lost in thought" (daydreaming): 62 percent
2. Cell phone use (talking, listening, dialing, texting): 12 percent
3. Paying attention to an outside person, object, or event: 7 percent
4. Interacting with other occupants: 5 percent
5. Using or reaching for a device in the vehicle, such as a portable GPS system or headphones: 2 percent
6. Eating or drinking: 2 percent
7. Adjusting audio or climate controls: 2 percent
8. Operating other in-vehicle devices, such as adjusting the rearview mirrors, seats, or using a built-in navigation system: 1 percent
9. Moving object in vehicle, such as an insect or unrestrained pet: 1 percent
10. Smoking-related (smoking, lighting up, putting ashes in ashtray): 1 percent

The cognitive distractions of cell phone use and thinking or daydreaming accounted for the most fatalities, and the insurance company analysts warn that even these may be underrep-

Among the most common activities while driving, smoking has been proven to be dangerously distracting.

resented, since in many fatal accidents police may not be able to determine what caused the crash. But even for the distractions at the bottom of the list—those at just 1 or 2 percent—the statistics represent at least 650 deaths. When nonfatal accidents are considered, especially those involving serious injuries, the human toll in suffering and disability would obviously be much higher.

The Little Things That Matter Inside the Vehicle

In Boston in 2013, it was a momentary glance at a GPS device that injured multiple people. Forty-two Pennsylvania high school students and chaperones were on a charter bus that had taken them for a visit to Harvard University and its surroundings. It was a pleasant day trip for the students, but as they were leaving the area to return home, the bus driver, sixty-seven-year-old Samuel J. Jackson, got confused driving on the Boston streets. He ended up on the wrong street, across which was a low overpass. Traffic signs warned that the bridge had a clearance of only 10 feet (3m) and that only cars were allowed on the road. Jackson did not see the signs; allegedly, he was looking at his GPS to try to figure out the correct route out of Boston. When he looked up and saw the bridge, it was too late. The bus slammed into the overpass and was severely damaged. Some students were trapped inside the bus for more than an hour until firefighters could get them out of the vehicle. Thirty-five students were injured, two seriously. The accident was traumatic for everyone. One of the organizers of the trip said, "There was a lot of glass, a lot of screaming, a lot of crying."[43] Fortunately, no one was killed in the accident, but it is an example of the visual and cognitive distraction that can put lives at risk. The bus driver's failure to see the warning signs may have been an example of inattention blindness, as he tried to think about navigating Boston's unfamiliar streets.

JUST DON'T EAT!

"Concentrating on eating can be just as distracting as texting while driving. Drivers need to keep not only their hands on the wheel; they also have to keep their brains on the road."—Marcel Just, Carnegie Mellon University professor and distracted driving expert

Quoted in Gina Roberts-Grey. "The 10 Worst Foods to Eat While Driving." MSN Money, February 17, 2011. http://money.msn.com/auto-insurance/the-10-worst-foods-to-eat -while-driving.aspx?cp-documentid=6788363.

Inattention blindness probably played a large role in Tiffany Ketner's 2014 accident, when she was one of those people distracted by an insect in her car. The insect was a bee that flew from the back of her car right in front of her face. Ketner is allergic to bees, and she was so distracted by the bee's presence that she failed to see the car stopped in front of her on the roadway waiting to make a turn. She slammed into the rear of the car ahead, and although she was not one of the 1 percent who are killed by an insect distraction, she was seriously injured. She suffered a cracked eye socket and broken bones in her face. The man in the vehicle she hit had a concussion and injured one arm. Ketner knew the accident was her fault. She said, "It's not their fault that I hit him. I just didn't see it." She wanted people to understand that she was not careless or uncaring. She felt terrible about causing the accident. She told the media about the bee, hoping, she said that she "could make people see I wasn't a monster."[44] Still, neither her eyes nor her brain could see past the distraction of the bee.

Distractions Outside the Vehicle

Distractions inside the car are bad enough, but they are not as frequent a cause of accidents as distractions outside the car. These distractions are usually the visual distractions that take the driver's eyes completely off the road during a moment when full attention to the road is necessary. Two frightening accidents on the Bay Bridge in Maryland illustrate how risky visual inattention can be. Maryland's Chesapeake Bay Bridge is an unusual stretch of roadway. At 4.3 miles (6.9k) long, it is the world's longest span over water, and it is heavily traveled and congested with traffic. Maryland police say that accidents on the bridge are increasing over time.

In April 2013, one accident involved a distracted driver just looking at the water and scenery. That driver collided with another car and pushed it into the bridge wall. In July of that same year, a tractor-trailer driver saw flashing lights behind him and wondered what was happening. He stared into his side mirror for so long that he failed to notice cars stopping in front of him in his lane. By the time he looked back at the roadway, it was too late to stop. He slammed into the car ahead with such force

Beautiful scenery—such as that seen from the Chesapeake Bay Bridge in Maryland—can be distracting for drivers. Police say accidents on the bridge have increased over time.

that the car was pushed over the bridge barrier and sent flying 27 feet (8.2m) down into the bay below. Then the tractor-trailer hit a third car before coming to a stop. Luckily, no one was badly injured in the frightening crash. The driver of the car that ended up in the bay was able to get out of her car and swim to a nearby abutment at the end of the bridge. Maryland police chief Michael Kundrat was angry about the distracted driving that almost caused a tragedy. He said, "This crash demonstrates how critical it is that motorists devote their full attention to driving when operating motor vehicles. Both the April and July crashes were a direct result of distracted driving. Every one of us has immense responsibility behind the wheel."[45]

It Is Not Funny

Any activity that takes any of a driver's attention away from driving is a distraction. As interest in the risk of distractions increases, more information becomes available about more distractions.

A dog in the car, especially on the front seat, can be distracting for the driver.

For example, in a survey conducted by AAA, researchers found that 19 percent of dog owners admit to taking their hands off the steering wheel to keep the pet from climbing into the front seat with them. Even more—52 percent—say that they have petted their dog while driving. AAA points out that such manual and often visual distractions increase the risk of an accident.

In another survey in 2014, the marketing company DME-automotive determined the top most common distractions that people engage in while driving. This survey was not about the top distractions that cause fatalities or crashes. Instead, it yielded the top five non-driving-related activities for all drivers. The top five activities are:

1. Singing out loud: 56 percent
2. Phone conversations: 50 percent
3. Eating: 50 percent
4. Reading a text message: 26 percent
5. Sending a text message: 20 percent

Is singing really a risky distracting activity? Mike Martinez, the chief marketing officer for DMEautomotive, says that it is.

He explains, "Drivers are pretty distracted; you have to close your eyes to hit the high notes." Martinez is worried about any inattention when people are behind the wheel. He adds, "It's a vehicle of disaster without constant vigilance. Even singing can take your attention away from the road. These things are funny, but there's a deadly serious aspect to it. You are responsible for a machine hurtling down the highway at 65 mph that requires 100 percent of your attention 100 percent of the time."[46]

The Worst Distraction: Mind Wandering

No matter how many different activities people perform while driving, however, the top cause of fatal accidents and dangerous distractions does not involve a device or an object. It is not manual or visual but cognitive, involving the mind and brain. The worst distraction of all, say researchers, may be daydreaming or being lost in thought. Experts refer to this as mind wandering. This distraction played a role in more than 60 percent of the fatal accidents analyzed by the Erie Insurance Company. It appears to be more dangerous than texting or phone conversations or any other momentary distraction behind the wheel.

Mind wandering is a normal condition of every human's brain. William Hampton, a writer for *Popular Mechanics*, explains that daydreaming is a natural function of the way the brain is wired and occurs frequently in all drivers. He says,

> Because millions of sensations bombard us every second, the brain sorts through them to allow only the most important ones to become conscious—for instance, you don't notice what's in your peripheral vision unless something moves there. It's just the way the brain evolved to protect it from self-destructing. If it allowed too many sensations to get through, we would be paralyzed by the massive sensory overload. The downside to this is that your mind has a narrow attention span, so it likes to wander—a lot. . . . Daydreaming can't be eliminated, only minimized.[47]

Tips to Reduce Mind Wandering

Mind wandering cannot be completely eliminated, but psychologist Paul Atchley of the University of Kansas suggests some tips that can help drivers stay alert. First, he says, people should remind themselves as they get in their cars that driving is risky. He explains, "If you approach driving as the potentially dangerous task that it really is, you're much more likely to pay attention." Next, do something to cue the brain not to "zone out" in the car. For example, a driver could put a colorful string or sticker on the dashboard as a reminder to stay alert. Third, drivers need to keep driving interesting. Drivers might entertain themselves by watching other drivers to see if they are using turn signals, weaving on the road, or acting distracted. This activity helps drivers to pay attention, look for potential risks, and drive defensively. Finally, if passengers are in the car, drivers should seek their help. Atchley says, "Passengers tend to look for threats, but will sometimes stay quiet because they don't want to be a backseat driver. If someone's riding with you, tell her to speak up if she sees something." All of these strategies help drivers focus instead of thinking about other things.

Quoted in Marygrace Taylor. "The Driving Habit You Need to Break." *Prevention*, December 2012. www .prevention.com/health/healthy-living/daydreaming -and-driving-can-cause-accidents.

People are especially prone to mind wandering when they are driving a familiar route or driving a long stretch of unvarying road. Their minds wander away from the task while their brains put the task of driving on automatic. Under these circumstances, drivers believe that they are aware of the environment, but they are not completely conscious of it. Their visual attention narrows, and they suffer from inattention blindness because their conscious thoughts are elsewhere. They are less attentive to the external world.

Evidence That Mind Wandering Affects Driving

In 2013, psychologists Matthew R. Yanko and Thomas M. Spalek used a driving simulator to study the effects of mind wandering on driving skills and performance. In this experiment, seventeen college students drove around a 7.5-mile (12k) oval track following a pace car. At random times, the pace car would apply its brakes and slow down. Then it would accelerate again. The study subjects had to quickly apply their own brakes in response to avoid hitting the pace car. The scientists also played a tone inside the vehicle at various times. Whenever the drivers heard the tone, they were asked to push one button if they believed their minds were on task or a second button if they felt their minds had been wandering (if they were thinking about things other than driving). At the end of the study, Yanko and Spalek compared the drivers' braking times when they were attending to driving and when they were mind wandering. The subjects reported mind wandering about 39 percent of the time. During those times, they took longer to brake in response to the pace car's braking. In other words, brake reaction time was decreased in comparison to their reaction times when they reported being on task. The drivers were slower to react to a possible emergency when they were mind wandering. Perhaps surprisingly, the researchers also discovered that the students drove faster when their minds were wandering than they did when they reported paying attention only to driving.

In a second experiment, Yanko and Spalek used a similar simulation with thirty-two subjects, but they measured how closely the drivers followed the pace car or how much distance they maintained between their own cars and the pace car. At one point in the experiment, the researchers also added a woman on the side of the road, walking forward to step out into the roadway. In this study, drivers reported mind wandering about 42 percent of the time. The woman was in the peripheral vision of the drivers. When the drivers reported mind wandering, they followed the pace car significantly more closely than they did when their minds were on task. In addition, they were slower to brake for the woman stepping into the road when their attention was not on driving. Yanko and Spalek say, "Avoiding obstacles and responding appropriately to emergencies are important goals when driving. It follows then that mind-wandering would impair a driver's ability to respond to these hazards."[48] With their studies, the researchers have found evidence that mind wandering leads to a form of inattention blindness, a reduced awareness of the driving environment, and less concern about maintaining a margin of safety on the road.

Ultimate Irony

"My father's brother was a pilot, and they rented a two-seater plane to take aerial shots. . . . The engine stalled, the plane crashed. My uncle died and my father survived. And I think, 'My god, my father survives a plane crash, but it is a water bottle that [later] kills him.'"—Karen Torres, the daughter of a victim struck and killed by a truck driver distracted by a dropped water bottle

Quoted in Erika Karp. "Miller Place Woman Takes Distracted Driving to Heart." *Village Beacon Record*, June 20, 2012. www.northshoreoflongisland.com/Articles-Features-i-2012 -06-21-92874.112114-sub-Miller-Place-woman-takes-distracted-driving-to-heart.html.

The Driver Is to Blame

In an Australian study of car accidents that caused injury, Vanessa Beanland and her research team analyzed 340 cases in which either a driver or the passenger had been interviewed about what led to the crash. The analysis covered all crashes in which at least one person was hospitalized between the years of 2000 and 2011. The researchers reported that the majority of the serious injury crashes involved some kind of distraction. They also concluded that 70 percent of the distractions that had caused the accidents were voluntary, meaning that they could have been prevented by the drivers. That means if the distractions were preventable, perhaps the accidents were, too.

Preventing distractions that could lead to accidents has been the strategy of UPS driver Tom Camp for fifty-one years. That is how long Camp has been a driver for UPS, and he has done so without ever having an accident. Camp says that 90 percent of

According to a veteran UPS driver, the key to staying safe on the road is to always pay attention.

staying safe on the road is "paying attention." He also tries to stay completely aware of what other drivers are doing and to drive defensively. He attempts to avoid changing lanes, leaves plenty of space between his truck and cars ahead of him, and never drives aggressively. Camp advises, "Stay focused. . . . Assume other drivers are not as aware as you are. If you assume the other guy is daydreaming, that's a good first step."[49]

Jeffrey Coben is an emergency room physician who has treated too many victims of vehicle accidents. He says that the injuries he sees are rarely the result of freak accidents, such as lightning striking a vehicle or tornadoes tossing a car. And they rarely happen because a vehicle's brakes fail or because of some other mechanical failure in the car. He insists, "Vehicle injuries are not accidents. They are predictable and preventable. Every crash is an interaction between an individual operating the vehicle and the environment it's in."[50] And, Coben says, every distracted individual driving a motor vehicle increases the risk of a crash and injury, both to himself or herself and to others.

Preventing Distracted Driving

Cambria Lee Gordon was a California woman living the good life. She was a mother of three and married to successful television producer Howard Gordon, who created the hit series *24* and *Homeland*. She was a respected environmental activist and children's author. Then, on July 20, 2011, her life changed in an instant. Gordon was driving down a street in Santa Monica when her cell phone fell to the floor of her SUV. As she reached to pick up her phone, she glanced away from the road, and when she looked back up, she saw a man crossing the street directly in front of her car. She tried to hit her brakes, but lost control of the car and hit eighty-two-year-old William Smerling. Gordon was horrified. She says that in that moment two thoughts ran through her head. She thought, "I hope he's okay," and "my life will change forever."[51]

Deadly Consequences

The pedestrian was terribly injured. He was rushed to the hospital while Gordon was interviewed by police and given a sobriety test. Gordon was frightened, emotionally distraught, and ashamed. She was completely sober and had not been speeding, but she was still holding her phone. She remembers, "Because I had the phone in my hand, it was a crime. And for the first time, I heard the words distracted driving, and I was a criminal." Smerling remained in the hospital for a month with multiple broken bones and internal injuries. Doctors did their best for him, but he later died of his injuries. Gordon was grief-stricken

71

and full of guilt, anxiety, and remorse. She says, "I could not believe that I had taken another person's life."[52]

The terrible event seemed to turn Gordon's life upside down. She was legally charged with misdemeanor and vehicular manslaughter without gross negligence. Months later, in court, Gordon admitted that she had made a tragic mistake and pleaded no contest to the charges. She also wrote a letter of apology to the court, in which she told of her deep regret for her actions. The letter ended, "Although I cannot presume to ask for forgiveness, I only hope that the Smerling family understands how immeasurably sorry I am."[53] She did not go to jail, but the judge in her case ordered her to be put on probation for three years and required her to perform 360 hours of community service related to education about distracted driving.

ALL ELECTRONIC DEVICES MUST GO

"Safety advocates, like the National Transportation Safety Board and the NSC, say that nothing short of a total ban on device use by drivers will stop the dangers of distracted drivers."—blog editor Payton Chung

Payton Chung. "Flawed Handheld Phone Bans Don't Stop Distracted Driving." *Streetsblog USA*, April 2, 2014. http://usa.streetsblog.org/2014/04/02/flawed-handheld -phone-bans-dont-stop-distracted-driving.

Gordon's life did change permanently after the accident. She now speaks at schools and other community groups about the dangers of distracted driving, and although she feels ashamed of her actions, she forces herself to tell her personal story as a warning to others. In 2014, she also decided to help found the nonprofit organization Partnership to End Distracted Driving, in an educational effort to fight all kinds of distracted driving. She is hopeful about the future. She says, "The thing that surprised me the most is how much talking about my accident publicly has helped me heal. If someone in the audience has heard my message then I've saved a life."[54]

Legal Efforts to Prevent Distracted Driving

Because distracted driving is a deadly serious issue, there is a strong private and public effort to make everyone aware of the problem and to end the worst kinds of distracted behaviors that put people in danger on the roads. Just as in Cambria Gordon's case, the goal is to save lives. The two main approaches to the prevention of distracted driving are legal and educational. In the United States, many state governments have attempted to tackle the issue with laws about the worst and most common kinds of distractions behind the wheel.

As of 2014, forty-four states, along with the District of Columbia, Puerto Rico, Guam, and the U.S. Virgin Islands, ban

Florida governor Rick Scott shakes hands with Florida Highway Patrol officers at a 2013 event in which he signed legislation banning texting while driving.

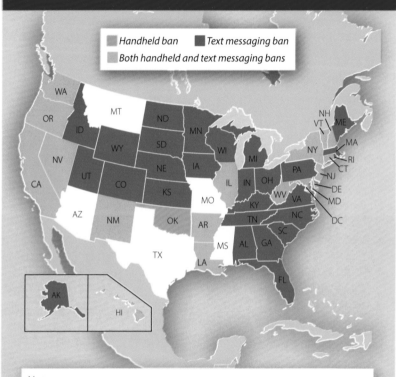

STATE LAWS BANNING CELL PHONE USE OR TEXTING WHILE DRIVING

■ Handheld ban   ■ Text messaging ban
■ Both handheld and text messaging bans

Notes:

Arkansas: For 18- to 20-year-olds; has also banned the use of handheld cell phones while driving in a school zone or in a highway construction zone for all drivers.

Louisiana: Learner or intermediate license (regardless of age).

New Hampshire: Effective July 2015.

New Mexico: In-state vehicles.

Oklahoma: Learner or intermediate license.

Texas: Has banned the use of handheld phones and texting in school zones.

Vermont: Effective October 2014.

Source: Governors Highway Safety Association, "Distracted Driving Laws," August 2014. www.ghsa.org/html/stateinfo/laws/cellphone_laws.html.

text messaging for all drivers. In all but five of these states, the ban is a primary enforcement law. Primary enforcement means that police can stop and ticket anyone that they see performing the behavior. Secondary enforcement laws, such as those in the five states without primary enforcement, are those in which police can issue a citation only if the driver is first caught committing another motor vehicle infraction. For example, if a driver runs a stop sign (primary enforcement law), the police officer can issue a secondary citation for texting if the driver was texting when he or she ran the stop sign. Of the six states that do not ban texting for every driver, only Montana has no law at all, and its state government expects to consider such legislation in 2015. Other states have laws that allow limited texting. South Carolina, for example, allows texting with hands-free technology or while legally stopped, for instance on the side of the road. In Oklahoma and Mississippi, on the other hand, new drivers, those with learning permits, and bus drivers are banned from texting.

In addition to banning texting, thirteen states, plus the District of Columbia, Puerto Rico, Guam, and the U.S. Virgin Islands, ban handheld cell phone use while driving, and thirty-seven states ban all cell phone use for new or teen drivers. In every state, whether or not there is a law about cell phone use, drivers who get into an accident can be cited for talking or texting because of existing laws about distracted driving, reckless driving, and negligent driving. In Canada, laws about handheld electronic devices are similar to those in the United States. People can be fined for any messaging or communication in every province except in the most northerly, mainly Inuit province of Nunavut. In Ontario, even if drivers are using hands-free devices, they can be charged with careless driving and fined if police determine their driving is endangering others. Around the world, many countries are even more restrictive than North America. In most European countries, handheld cell phone use while driving is illegal, and in Japan, both handheld and hands-free phone use are banned.

Are Distracted Driving Laws Beneficial?

Around the world, laws restricting the use of devices for texting and talking are justified by the presumption that such laws make the roadways safer for everyone by reducing distracted driving. In the United States, however, some people question whether bans on cell phone use or texting really work. Evidence does exist that laws can make a difference. In California, for example, handheld cell phone use while driving was banned in 2008. In 2012, the California Office of Traffic Safety released a report that compared fatal vehicle accidents that occurred before and after the 2008 law. The study, from a research team at the University of California, Berkeley, looked at fatal crashes in the two years before 2008 and the traffic fatalities two years after the law was enacted. It demonstrated that traffic deaths as a whole were reduced by 22 percent after 2008 and that driver deaths blamed on handheld cell phone use had dropped by 47 percent. David Ragland, the director of the research, said, "These results suggest that the law banning hand-held cell phone use while driving had a positive impact on reducing traffic fatalities and injuries."[55]

In a telephone survey conducted in 2009, researchers Keli A. Braitman and Anne T. McCartt compared states with bans against handheld phone use in vehicles to states without such laws. They discovered that 56 percent of respondents admitted to phone use while driving in states that banned drivers from using handheld phones. But 69 percent of respondents in states without bans used their phones while driving. The use of hands-free phones also increased in the states with laws banning driving with handheld phones. These results seem to suggest that laws banning handheld phones help to reduce the use of the phones for some drivers.

In another study from 2012, Cheng Cheng, a professor at Texas A&M University, found that in states where texting and handheld phone use are illegal, drivers texted 60 percent less and talked on handheld phones 40 percent less than in states without such laws. When the state of Florida outlawed texting and driving in 2013, governor Rick Scott argued, "Just the fact

The Determined Distracted Driving Expert

Jennifer Smith is one of the most active advocates in the United States against the dangers of distracted driving. She is a speaker and lecturer who shares the science and research about distracted driving with anyone who will listen. She shares her personal story, too. Smith lost her mother to distracted driving in 2008. She says,

> My mother . . . was leaving her neighborhood when a 20-year-old driver t-boned her car at 45-50 mph, he never saw the red light or the other cars already stopped at that light, he never saw my mom's car until it was too late, and he never even tried to brake. The first thing he said when he

got out of his car was that he was talking on the phone and he never saw my mom right in front of him. He was not texting, he was not dialing, he was not looking for his phone. He was doing what hundreds of thousands of people do every day, maybe even you, having a conversation while driving.

Since that tragedy, Smith has educated herself and tirelessly worked with the U.S. Department of Transportation, Oprah Winfrey, and even the United Nations in campaigns to end distracted driving.

Jennifer Smith. "About Jennifer." Jennifer Smith: Distracted Driving Advocate and Speaker. http://jennifer smith-distracteddriving.com/About_Jennifer.html.

Jennifer Smith (left) speaks at a news conference on distracted driving at the U.S. Department of Transportation in Washington, D.C., in January 2010.

that it'll be illegal to text and drive, I think that's going to stop our teenagers, stop citizens from texting and driving."[56]

Are Such Laws Really Enough?

When researchers try to accurately measure the effectiveness of laws prohibiting phone use and texting, however, the results are much less clear than lawmakers and citizens might wish. The bad news from the study by Keli Braitman and Anne McCartt, for instance, is that the majority of drivers in states that ban handheld phones use them anyway. A lot of people do not take the laws seriously or believe that they can get away with breaking the law. In Canada, where handheld phone use while driving has been illegal since 2012, 52 percent of drivers use their cell phones anyway. Canadian police officer Tom O'Brien says, "It's still a problem. We don't catch nearly as many of those that

New York governor Andrew Cuomo speaks at a news conference to announce increased penalties for texting and driving in 2013.

are out there doing it."[57] Enforcement of cell phone laws can be problematic. Often, people notice a police cruiser and put down their phones so that they will not be caught. When police are not around, people ignore the law.

Texting and driving laws are hard to enforce, too. In the six months after Pennsylvania banned texting and driving in 2012, for instance, police in the city of Scranton wrote fewer than ten citations. This low number was not due to police disinterest, but to the difficulty of enforcing the law. Scranton police chief Carl Graziano explained, "It's difficult to make that arrest due to the current law. It's difficult for an officer to discern whether they're texting or looking up numbers on their phone."[58] (Pennsylvania does not have laws banning cell phone use.) In a 2012 survey of drivers in New York, researchers actually discovered that the percentage of people who text while driving had increased since the practice was outlawed, perhaps only because more people have smartphones than they did before the law was in place.

Effectiveness Unproven

The effectiveness of laws banning texting and cell phone use in increasing safety on the roads and reducing accidents is not easy to determine. When researchers attempt to assess the practical value of such laws, their results are mixed. Some studies suggest that strong laws, diligently enforced, do reduce traffic accidents and collisions. Other studies show no effect or even a decrease in safety as measured by collisions and accidents. In one 2011 study, researchers looked at insurance claims for damaged cars in California, Connecticut, New York, and the District of Columbia. They compared insurance claims before and after bans took effect in each area. In California and the District of Columbia, a small reduction in claims was noted, suggesting that the bans may have reduced accidents from cell phone use. But in Connecticut and New York, the researchers found small increases in collision claims after the bans were passed. In another study in 2013, researchers found no difference in the rate of car crashes before and after cell phone laws were passed in the

Lives Still at Risk

In 2014 the U.S. Centers for Disease Control and Prevention reported that teens are not smoking cigarettes as much as in the past. They are not drinking and driving, and even their use of alcohol in general has declined since 2011. But 41 percent have texted or e-mailed while driving. About 60 percent of high school seniors admit to having texted while driving. The behavior is now perhaps the riskiest activity that teens engage in, and it is one of the most dangerous and deadly things any driver can do.

Texting while driving is perhaps currently the riskiest activity in which teens commonly engage.

District of Columbia, New York, New Jersey, Connecticut, and Chicago, Illinois. In national studies of fatal crashes after texting bans are enacted, a few of them report decreased fatalities, but a few more actually report an increase in fatalities after texting laws are passed.

In 2013, two University of Wisconsin, Milwaukee researchers presented evidence that texting bans increase driver safety only temporarily. Scott Adams and Rahi Abouk reported that such bans work at first, when the law is new, to reduce the number of crashes. Then, after a few months, the change in safety disappears. Adams says, "This is suggestive of drivers reacting to the announcement of the legislation, only to return to old habits shortly afterward." People go back to texting and driving once they feel sure that they can get away with it and maybe because drivers feel so dependent on their phones. Also, perhaps, in cases where crashes increase, it is because drivers are trying to hide their phones while they are texting and so they are more visually and manually distracted than when they used their phones in plain sight. For example, in Washington State, which enacted a texting ban in 2007, people took the law seriously at first and stopped texting while driving. Therefore, crashes were reduced. However, in every year since the first year, the effectiveness of the law has been reduced more and more, and accidents and texting increased again. Such results are frustrating for researchers, who know how dangerous distracted driving can be. Adams says, "What we need is to find a way to take this as seriously as drunk driving because enforcement has shown to have an effect on fatalities caused by drunk driving."[59]

Scientists know that cell phone use and texting are just as risky as drunk driving, but enforcement of laws may not be enough to put an end to distracted driving. People's attitudes must change. Governments, private foundations, and concerned individuals devote much energy to education and persuasion in the hope that people will listen and believe in the serious threat of distracted driving. Perhaps then and only then will drivers put an end to their risky behaviors behind the wheel.

Protecting Teens: Public Awareness and the Law

Donna Weeks is one of the individuals trying to put an end to driving distractions—and not just those involving phones and texting, but all distractions, especially for young people. In December 2006, Weeks lost her daughter Kyleigh D'Alessio in a terrible crash that changed her family's life forever. Kyleigh, who was sixteen at the time, was a passenger in a car driven by seventeen-year-old Tanner Birch and carrying two other teen passengers. Tanner had a provisional driver's license, which is a restricted license granted to new and teen drivers. In the state of New Jersey, where the teens all lived, this provisional license meant that Tanner was not allowed to have multiple underage passengers in his car. No one knows exactly why the accident happened, but teen passengers are known to increase the risk of teen driver distraction. Tanner lost control of his vehicle that day, left the road, and smashed head-on into a tree. Both Tanner and Kyleigh were killed in the crash, and the other two passengers were injured.

In the midst of her grief over losing Kyleigh so tragically, Donna Weeks became determined to try to save other parents and their children from suffering the same fate that she had. For the next three years after her daughter's death, Weeks lobbied her state legislature to pass more restrictive laws to protect new drivers in New Jersey. In 2010, New Jersey's state government passed "Kyleigh's Law." The law made New Jersey the first state in the nation to require red decals to be placed on the vehicles of new drivers. These decals make the new teen driver obvious to police, who then can observe the car and pull the driver over for any infraction of the rules associated with a provisional or probationary license. During their first year of driving in New Jersey, for example, probationary and provisional drivers may not carry more than one passenger nor use any electronic device or drive after 11 P.M. Weeks and the New Jersey legislature hope

A decal denoting a motorist under the age of twenty-one is seen on a New Jersey license plate at a ceremony to implement Kyleigh's Law in 2010. The law is named for Kyleigh D'Alessio, a sixteen-year-old student killed in a vehicle driven by another teen.

that the red decals on the vehicles will save teen lives by allow-
ing strict police enforcement of the probationary rules. Many
people objected to Kyleigh's Law, but Weeks responded, "I wish
people would just let it run its course and let's see what it does.
I know we cannot save everybody. I know car accidents happen.
But there are just so many senseless, preventable ones, and the
least amount of teens in a car, the better off we'll be."[60]

Weeks did not stop with her advocacy for teen driver safety
when Kyleigh's Law was successfully passed. She partnered with
the National Safety Council's HEARTS Network and the New
Jersey Teen Safe Driving Coalition to try to spread the word to
teens and their parents about the dangers of distracted driving. HEARTS stands for "Honoring Everyone Affected, Rallying
The Survivors," and its goal is to collect and tell personal stories about teen car accidents for teens, parents, and educators.
HEARTS' leaders believe that stories are as helpful as laws at in-
fluencing young drivers and their parents to reject unsafe behaviors behind the wheel. Weeks has contributed articles and her
own story to HEARTS. She tries to help other coalitions in other
states, as well as in New Jersey, to set up graduated driver licens-
ing (provisionary and probationary) programs for new drivers.
She says, "It is time we start to make a difference, knowing now
after so much research that a high percentage of these crashes
are preventable. I hope this generation of teen drivers is more
aware of the dangers it faces and is the one that will accept these
changes for themselves and their friends, and make these tragedies a thing of the past."[61]

Campaigning Against Distracted Driving

Telecommunications giant AT&T began a distracted driving
campaign of its own in 2009. The company has spent millions
of dollars to persuade drivers to put down their phones and
pledge not to text and drive with its "It Can Wait" initiative.
The campaign strives to educate people about the dangers of
texting and driving with advertising on television, Facebook,
Twitter, and YouTube. Together with other telecommunications

A man sits in a texting and driving simulator as part of a June 2014 "It Can Wait" event sponsored by AT&T in New York City.

companies like Verizon, T-Mobile, and Sprint, campaign leaders stage events in communities around the country to persuade people to take the pledge not to text and drive. For instance, they hold assemblies at schools or set up a driving simulator at colleges where students can experience for themselves the dangers of texting and driving. On the Internet, It Can Wait offers a driving simulator game that anyone can play to discover how badly he or she drives while texting. AT&T executive vice president Cathy Coughlin is the leader of the It Can Wait campaign, and she is passionate about it. She says, "Seventy-five percent of Americans have heard the message on the dangers of texting and driving. But we haven't gotten 75 percent of Americans to stop texting and driving. Now we have to move the needle on behavior. We're going to stay after this."[62]

SAFETY TIP

"Use #X as a signal that you're driving. [Texting] #X lets friends know that you're getting on the road and can't respond. It can also mean you're ending a text string until you're done driving."—AT&T It Can Wait campaign

AT&T Texting & Driving . . . It Can Wait. "Tips & Tools." www.itcanwait.com.

In April 2014, the U.S. Department of Transportation (DOT) launched its first national advertising campaign to begin National Distracted Driving Awareness Month. With advertisements on television, radio, and the Internet, the DOT aimed to fight texting and driving, in particular, and to persuade people to focus on driving and put down any electronic devices. The DOT asks people to turn off electronic devices when they get behind the wheel, to be good role models for others when they drive, and to speak up as passengers if a driver uses a phone or other device.

Please, Listen and Learn

No matter how many laws are passed or how much education is made available to the public, the menace of distracted driving cannot be stopped until every individual takes it seriously. Terry L. Mathis, a safety expert, asks that each driver think of the acronym "ACE" when getting behind the wheel. "A" stands for attention, meaning keeping the brain focused and avoiding cognitive distraction. "C" is for control, and represents avoiding manual distraction by never taking a hand off the steering wheel. "E" stands for keeping one's eyes on the road and eliminating visual distraction.

Michael Richards is one distracted driving victim who pleads for everyone to take the dangers seriously. While driving his truck one day, he looked down at his phone for 1.7 seconds to read a two-word text message, lost control and flipped his vehicle, and mangled and lost his arm in the crash. Richards says he thought he was too smart and too capable to suffer for his inattention, but he was wrong. He says, "I want young people to stand up to their parents or peers and tell them not to text and drive. And, I want adults to do the same. The message is: Don't take your life, or the lives of others nearby, into your hands by being distracted for even one second. If that message helps save just one person, then I'm happy."[63] Distracted driving is just not worth the risk.

NOTES

Introduction: A Deadly Epidemic

1. U.S. Department of Transportation. "U.S. Transportation Secretary Ray LaHood Responds to Misleading Distracted Driving Study." Briefing Room press release, September 28, 2010. www.dot.gov/briefing-room/us-transportation-sec retary-ray-lahood-responds-misleading-distracted-driving -study.

2. Leon Krolikowski, submitted to Michael Dinan. "Police Chief: Distracted Driving 'A New Traffic Safety Epidemic' in New Canaan." *New Canaanite*, June 19, 2014. http:// newcanaanite.com/police-chief-distracted-driving-a-new -traffic-safety-epidemic-in-new-canaan-5547.

3. Quoted in Ray Kisonas. "Deadly Distraction: A Woman Was Killed, the Teenage Driver Charged, but Forgiveness Has Hollowed." *Monroe News*, October 24, 2013. www.monroe news.com/news/2013/oct/25/deadly-distraction.

4. Quoted in Kisonas. "Deadly Distraction."

Chapter 1: What Is Distracted Driving?

5. Quoted in Kendra Nichols. "Crash Survivor Shares Story to Discourage Distracted Driving," ABC27.com, July 25, 2012. www.abc27.com/story/19114617/survivor-injured -while-texting-and-driving-tells-story.

6. Quoted in Monica Von Dobeneck. "Distracted Driving Cost Her an Eye and Led to Multiple Surgeries, a Woman Tells Central Penn College Students." PennLive.com, July 25, 2012. www.pennlive.com/midstate/index.ssf/2012/07/dis tracted_driving_cost_her_an.html.

7. Distraction.gov. "What Is Distracted Driving?" www.dis traction.gov/content/get-the-facts/facts-and-statistics .html.

8. Quoted in Lucia Huntington. "The Real Distraction at the Wheel." *Boston Globe*, October 14, 2009. www.boston.com /lifestyle/food/articles/2009/10/14/dining_while_driving _theres_many_a_slip_twixt_cup_and_lip_but_that _doesnt_stop_us/?page=1.

9. Quoted in James Turner. "Ex-Transit Driver Fined for Running Over Senior." *Winnipeg Free Press*, May 21, 2014. www .winnipegfreepress.com/local/daydream-cost-senior-his -leg-260066331.html?device=mobile.

10. Quoted in Eugene Buenaventura. "The Dangers of Eating and Driving." KAPP TV, February 20, 2013. www.kapptv .com/article/2013/feb/20/dangers-eating-driving.

11. Quoted in Matt Richtel. "In Study, Texting Lifts Crash Risk by Large Margin." *New York Times*, July 27, 2009. www.nytimes.com/2009/07/28/technology/28texting .html?pagewanted=all&_r=0.

12. Quoted in Ken Thomas, Associated Press. "Study: Distractions Cause Most Car Crashes." *Washington Post*, April 21, 2006. www.washingtonpost.com/wp-dyn/content/article /2006/04/21/AR2006042100568.html.

13. Quoted in Amber Hildebrandt. "Cellphones Blamed as Fatal Collisions by 'Distracted Drivers' Up." CBC News, August 19, 2013. www.cbc.ca/news/canada/cellphones-blam ed-as-fatal-collisions-by-distracted-drivers-up-1.1308025.

14. Distraction.gov. "Frequently Asked Questions." www.dis traction.gov/content/get-the-facts/faq.html.

15. Quoted in Steven D. Mackay. "*New England Journal of Medicine* Study: Virginia Tech Researchers Find Novice Teen Drivers Easily Fall into Distraction, Accidents." *Virginia Tech News*, January 2, 2014. www.vtnews.vt.edu/articles /2014/01/010214-vtti-nejm.html.

16. Sheila G. Klauer et al. "Distracted Driving and Risk of Road Crashes Among Novice and Experienced Drivers." *New England Journal of Medicine* 370:54–59 (January 2, 2014). www.nejm.org/doi/full/10.1056/NEJMsa1204142#t =article.

17. Quoted in Mackay. "*New England Journal of Medicine* study."

Chapter 2: Texting: The Scariest Distraction

18. Quoted in CBS Denver. "Parents Share Son's Final Text From Behind the Wheel." April 11, 2013. http://denver.cbs local.com/2013/04/11/final-text-before-deadly-car-crash.

19. Distraction.gov. "Frequently Asked Questions."

20. Quoted in Jane Shin Park. "The Real Risks of Texting and Driving." *Teen Vogue*, May 2013. www.teenvogue.com/ad vice/2013-05/texting-and-driving-teens.

21. Scott W. Campbell. "Why Do People (Still) Text and Drive?" *Huffington Post*, November 15, 2013. www.huffing tonpost.com/scott-w-campbell/why-do-people-still-text -_b_4269298.html.

22. Don't Text and Drive: Statistics. "DWI: Driving While Intoxicated." www.textinganddrivingsafety.com/texting-and -driving-stats.

23. Daniel V. McGehee. "Driving Young, Driving Distracted." *Huffington Post*, November 25, 2013. www.huffingtonpost .com/daniel-v-mcgehee-phd/driving-young-driving -dis_b_4317725.html.

24. Quoted in Marisela Burgos. "Teen Shares Story About the Dangers of Texting While Driving." Wave3 News, October 4, 2009. www.wave3.com/story/11256134/teen-shares-story -about-the-dangers-of-texting-while-driving.

25. Quoted in "NHTSA Survey Finds 660,000 Drivers Using Cell Phones or Manipulating Electronic Devices While Driving at Any Given Daylight Moment." U.S. Department of Transportation, April 5, 2013. www.dot.gov/briefing-room /nhtsa-survey-finds-660000-drivers-using-cell-phones-or -manipulating-electronic-devices.

26. Quoted in Sonari Glinton. "Distracted Driving: We're All Guilty, So What Should We Do About It?" NPR: All Tech Considered, November 11, 2012. www.npr.org/blogs/all techconsidered/2012/11/11/164876282/distracted-dri ving-were-all-guilty-so-what-should-we-do-about-it.

27. Quoted in "Hands-Free Talking, Texting Are Unsafe." News Center, University of Utah, June 12, 2013. http://unews .utah.edu/news_releases/hands-free-talking-texting-are -unsafe.

28. Quoted in Jon Hamilton. "Think You're Multitasking? Think Again." NPR, October 2, 2008. www.npr.org/templates /story/story.php?storyId=95256794.

29. Quoted in Laura Walter. "Multitasking and Distracted Driving: You Are Not the Exception." *EHS Today*, January 25, 2013. http://ehstoday.com/safety/multitasking-and -distracted-driving-you-are-not-exception.

30. Quoted in "Teen Turns Tragic Texting While Driving Accident into Inspirational Message for Others." WHAS11.com, November 19, 2009. www.whas11.com/news/Teen-turns -tragic-texting-while-driving-accident-into-inspirational -message-for-others-70544407.html.

31. Charlene Lake. "Texting While Driving: An Instant Can Change Your Life . . . Your Life Can Change in an Instant." *Huffington Post*, August 15, 2012. www.huffingtonpost.com /charlene-lake/texting-while-driving_b_1778738.html.

Chapter 3: Dangerous Phone Conversations

32. Quoted in Peter Meiszner. "Driver Reaching for Cell Phone Causes Four Vehicle Crash in North Vancouver." Global News, May 1, 2014. http://globalnews.ca/news/1305210 /driver-reaching-for-cell-phone-causes-four-vehicle-crash -in-north-vancouver.

33. Kiernan Hopkins. "Distracted Driver Causes Fatal Accident." DistractedDriverAccidents.com. http://distracteddri veraccidents.com/distracted-driver-fatal-accident.

34. Susan Yum. "Cell Phones and Driving Is the New Drunk Driving." *Huffington Post*, November 26, 2013. www.huf fingtonpost.com/susan-yum/cell-phones-and-driving-is -the-new-drunk-driving_b_4318421.html.

35. Quoted in Barry Simms. "Man Fined in Baltimore County Crash That Killed 5-year-old Boy." WBALTV.com, September 11, 2013. www.wbaltv.com/news/maryland/baltimore -county/man-fined-in-baltimore-county-crash-that-killed -5yearold-boy/21871400#!0TxKY.

36. National Safety Council. "Distracted Driving." Our Driving Concern: Employer Traffic Safety Program. www.nsc.org /safety_road/Employer%20Traffic%20Safety/Pages/Nation

alDistractedDriving.aspx.

37. Arien Mack. "Inattentional Blindness: Looking Without Seeing." *Current Directions in Psychological Science* vol. 12, no. 5 (October 2003): p. 180. www.unc.edu/~pcg/225 /documents/InattentionalBLindness2003.pdf.

38. David L. Strayer and Frank A. Drews. "Cell-Phone-Induced Driver Distraction." *Current Directions in Psychological Science* vol. 16, no. 3 (June 2007): p. 131. www.psych.utah .edu/lab/appliedcognition/publications/cellphone.pdf.

39. Judy Teater. "Remembering Joe Teater (Judy's son), April 12, 1991–January 20, 2004." FocusDriven.org. www.focus driven.org/our-board.

40. National Safety Council. "Understanding the Distracted Brain." White paper, March 2010, p. 6. www.nsc.org/safety _road/Distracted_Driving/Documents/Dstrct_Drvng _White_Paper_1_2011.pdf.

Chapter 4: All the Momentary Distractions

41. Allison E. Curry et al. "Peer Passengers: How Do They Affect Teen Crashes?" *Journal of Adolescent Health* vol. 50, no. 6 (June 2012): p. 592. Accessed at www.researchgate.net.

42. Quoted in Amanda Sergeyev and Samantha Mineroff. "Another Near-Disastrous Distracted Driving Story." *Bucks County Courier Times*, May 9, 2014. www.buckscountycou riertimes.com/life-style/reality/another-near-disastrous-dis tracted-driving-story/article_828d5c77-ac53-50ba-8db9 -9f5676e284f7.html.

43. Quoted in Associated Press. "After Harvard Visit, Dozens Injured in Bus Crash." *USA Today*, February 4, 2013. www .usatoday.com/story/news/nation/2013/02/02/bus-boston -crash-bridge/1886869.

44. Quoted in Becky Vargo. "Bee-Distracted Driver, Victim Discuss Crash." *Grand Haven Tribune*, June 14, 2014. www .grandhaventribune.com/article/policefire/1032461.

45. Quoted in Katie Lange. "MdTA: Distracted Driving Led to Bay Bridge Crash." WBALTV.com, August 30, 2013. www .wbaltv.com/news/maryland/anne-arundel-county/mdta -distracted-driving-led-to-bay-bridge-crash/21701044.

46. Quoted in Casey Williams. "Crooning While Cruising Tops Distracted Driving Charts." *Indianapolis Star*, April 18, 2014. www.indystar.com/story/money/2014/04/18/autos-croon ing-cruising-tops-distracted-driving-charts/7877749.

47. William Hampton, "Just How Dangerous Is Daydreaming While Driving?" *Popular Mechanics,* September 17, 2013. www.popularmechanics.com/cars/how-to/repair/just-how -dangerous-is-daydreaming-while-driving-15935216.

48. Matthew R. Yanko and Thomas M. Spalek. "Driving with the Wandering Mind: The Effect that Mind-Wandering Has on Driving Performance." *Human Factors: The Journal of the Human Factors and Ergonomics Society* (July 5, 2013): p. 2. Accessed at www.researchgate.net.

49. Quoted in Tammy Stables Battaglia, *Detroit Free Press.* "UPS driver has no crashes in 51 years." *USA Today*, No-vember 4, 2013. www.usatoday.com/story/money/business /2013/11/03/ups-driver-from-livonia-works-51-years-no -crashes/3426227.

50. Quoted in Nathan Seppa. "Impactful Distraction." *Science News*, August 9, 2013. www.sciencenews.org/article/impact ful-distraction.

Chapter 5: Preventing Distracted Driving

51. Quoted in Colette Wright. "Distracted Driver Shares Tragic Story." *La Puma*, March 17, 2014. www.chslapuma.com /news/2014/03/17/distracted-driver-shares-tragic-story.

52. Quoted in Maral Tavitian. "Lecture Warns Students About Dangers of Texting." *Daily Trojan*, February 24, 2014. http://dailytrojan.com/2014/02/24/lecture-warns-students -about-dangers-of-texting.

53. Quoted in "'Homeland'/'24' Creator's Wife Cops Plea in Driving Death 'I'm Immeasurably Sorry.'" TMZ.com, Feb-ruary 8, 2012. www.tmz.com/2012/02/08/cambria-howard -gordon-cops-plea-bargain-driving-death-cell-phone.

54. Quoted in Wright. "Distracted Driver Shares Tragic Story."

55. Quoted in Chris Cochran. "Cell Phone Distracted Driv-ing Deaths Down Since Laws Enacted." California Office of Traffic Safety, press release, March 5, 2012. www.ots

.ca.gov/Media_and_Research/Press_Room/2012/doc/Cell _Phone_deaths_down.pdf.

56. Quoted in Rochelle Koff and Gina Cherelus. "Rick Scott Signs Texting-While-Driving Ban, but Does It Have Teeth?" *Tampa Bay Times*, May 28, 2013. www.tampabay.com/news /politics/stateroundup/rick-scott-to-sign-texting-while -driving-ban-but-does-it-have-teeth/2123402.

57. Quoted in Bethany Cairns et al. "London Police Question Cellphone Ban's Effectiveness." Western Journalism: Project London, 2011. http://uwojournalism.squarespace.com/dri ven-to-distraction.

58. Quoted in Katie Sullivan. "Texting Laws Ineffective, Hard to Enforce, Police Say." *Times-Tribune*, September 4, 2012. http://thetimes-tribune.com/news/texting-laws-ineffective -hard-to-enforce-police-say-1.1367980.

59. Quoted in Laura L. Hunt. "Do Bans Curb Texting While Driving?" Today@UWM, June 4, 2013. www5.uwm.edu /news/2013/06/04/do-bans-curb-texting-while-driving /#.U7l-HdhOUdW.

60. Quoted in Jim Lockwood, *Star-Ledger*. "Kyleigh's Law Re- quires License Decals for Young N.J. Drivers." NJ.com, April 30, 2010. www.nj.com/news/index.ssf/2010/04/ky leighs_law_requiring_license.html.

61. Donna Weeks. "In Our Own Words—Donna Weeks." Teen Safe Driving, National Safety Council. http://teensafedriv ing.org/blog/in-our-own-words-donna-weeks-2.

62. Quoted in Cheryl Hall. "AT&T Spending Millions to Get It Can Wait Message Across." *Dallas Morning News*, Septem- ber 21, 2013. www.dallasnews.com/business/columnists /cheryl-hall/20130921-att-spending-millions-to-get-it -can-wait-message-across.ece.

63. Quoted in Jennifer Weston. "Michael Richards and Dis- tracted Driving." Moving Insider, March 31, 2014. http:// movinginsider.com/2014/03/31/distracted-driving-story.

Chapter 1: What Is Distracted Driving?

1. What experiences have you personally had with distracted driving? What kind of distraction was involved?

2. What might be some of the reasons that secondary tasks are more dangerous for novice drivers than for experienced drivers?

3. In what ways are distracted driving and drunk driving alike? How are they different?

Chapter 2: Texting: The Scariest Distraction

1. Would you be willing to text and drive? What if you had auto complete or voice-to-text technology? Would you be tempted?

2. How does brain function determine a person's ability to multitask?

3. Why do people text and drive even when they know it is dangerous? Have you heard any excuses and reasons from friends and family?

Chapter 3: Dangerous Phone Conversations

1. People often think that hands-free phone use while driving is safe. Why might they be wrong?

2. Can drivers tell when they are suffering with inattention blindness? Is it real, and do you think you could overcome it if you were driving and talking on the phone?

3. How do fMRI studies of the brain relate to real-world driving and phone use experiences?

Chapter 4: All the Momentary Distractions

1. Have you ever experienced mind wandering that reduced your awareness of your environment? What were the circumstances and what did you miss?

2. What are some of the ways that teen passengers might distract a teen driver? Have you ever seen such distraction in action?

3. Is there such a thing as a vehicle "accident" or is a crash always preventable by driver attention and focus?

Chapter 5: Preventing Distracted Driving

1. Are state laws that specifically restrict teen drivers fair? Why or why not?

2. What are the laws about distracted driving in your state? Do you think they are safe, effective, and fair?

3. Would you be willing to "take the pledge" not to text and drive? Why or why not?

ORGANIZATIONS TO CONTACT

AAA Foundation for Traffic Safety

607 Fourteenth Street, Suite 201
Washington, DC 20005
Phone: (202) 638-5944
Website: www.aaafoundation.org

The AAA Foundation's mission is to identify traffic safety issues, find solutions to those issues, and provide educational and informational resources to the public about driving safety.

FocusDriven

PO Box 45333
Omaha, NE 68145
Phone: (630) 775-2405
Website: www.focusdriven.org

FocusDriven is an advocacy organization dedicated to cell-phone-free driving. The organization seeks to put a human face on the suffering caused by phone use while driving in order to make the public aware of the real cost of distracted driving. It also supports victims and the families of victims of distracted driving by giving them a place to tell their stories and offering a series of workshops that teach victims and families how to educate their communities about the dangers of distracted driving.

Impact Teen Drivers

PO Box 161209
Sacramento, CA 95816
Phone: (916) 733-7432
Website: www.impactteendrivers.org

This California-based nonprofit organization is dedicated to fighting traffic fatalities, the leading cause of death in teens. It conducts school presentations nationwide in its "What Do You Consider Lethal?" campaign about reckless and distracted driving. Its ultimate goal is to reduce teen injuries and deaths caused by distracted driving and poor decision making behind the wheel.

National Highway Traffic Safety Administration (NHTSA)

1200 New Jersey Ave. SE, West Bldg.
Washington, DC 20590
Phone: (888) 327-4236
Website: www.nhtsa.gov

NHTSA offers information, education, and research on several key issues involving driving and vehicle safety. Its website on distracted driving is Distraction.gov (www.distraction.gov), where it invites visitors to get involved, spread the word, and take a pledge not to text and drive.

National Safety Council (NSC)

1121 Spring Lake Drive
Itasca, IL 60143
Phone: (800) 621-7615
Website: www.nsc.org

NSC has extensive information about safe driving and the dangers of distracted driving, especially involving cell phone use. Its educational materials include posters, fact sheets, and videos, all available free of charge.

Books

Lisa Creedon. *The Ride Guide: What You Don't Know CAN Hurt You!* Atlanta: Alcovy, 2013. This book is full of practical advice for vehicle safety, presented in an interesting, easy-to-read style. The author offers tips as various as how to avoid becoming a carjacking victim to how to know when a car needs repair to how to avoid accidents. She emphasizes defensive driving and learning how to know if you are a good driver.

Lauren Kennedy Smith. *Crash! What You Don't Know About Driving Can Kill You!* Victoria, BC, Canada: Friesen, 2012. Although written for adults, this reader-friendly book can help anyone to be a better driver. The author discusses such issues as distraction, focused awareness, aggressive driving, defensive driving, and the psychology of driving.

Stefan Kiesbye, ed. *Distracted Driving* (At Issue). Farmington Hills, MI: Greenhaven, 2012. Different opinions, from researchers, individuals, and safety experts, are presented about the issue of distracted driving and its impact and importance. Many kinds of distractions are discussed, including texting, phone conversations, passengers, and eating while driving.

Patricia D. Netzley. *How Serious Is Teen Drunk and Distracted Driving?* (In Controversy). San Diego: ReferencePoint, 2013. This book examines the serious topic of reckless and distracted driving with factual information and informed opinions. Its focus is on teens—what they are doing, what needs to be done to increase their safety, and whether more laws are needed to fight the problem.

Gail Stewart. *Cell Phones and Distracted Driving* (Cell Phones and Society). San Diego: ReferencePoint, 2014. The author concentrates specifically on how cell phones have affected driving habits in today's society. The book covers the science of distraction with cell phone use, laws about driving and cell phone use, and whether laws are working to change behavior.

Websites

AT&T The Last Text Documentary (www.schooltube.com /video/4386d84344d2a7345c5e/ATT-The-Last-Text-Docu mentary). Watch this ten-minute video of true stories of the tragedy that texting and driving can cause at SchoolTube. *The Last Text* is a moving and impactful look at some results of distracted driving.

Distraction.gov (www.distraction.gov). Get the facts on distracted driving, watch the videos, listen to the stories, and take the pledge. The slogan is "One text or call could wreck it all."

EndDD (www.enddd.org). Full of facts and information, this End Distracted Driving site also offers real stories about people whose lives were ended by distracted drivers. This site is sponsored by the Casey Feldman Foundation, which was established by Joel Feldman after his daughter Casey was killed by a distracted driver.

It Can Wait (www.itcanwait.com). This AT&T site is dedicated to ending texting and driving. It has tips for avoiding the behavior, free apps, and a driving simulator game that demonstrates the real consequences of texting while driving. How well can you do? AT&T says, "No text is worth dying for," and asks visitors to pledge never to text while driving.

Red Thumb Reminder (www.redthumbreminder.com). An ordinary citizen and father came up with a creative way to break his cell phone habit. Learn about it here. Visitors are invited to try the tactic themselves and share the story.

INDEX

PICTURE CREDITS

Cover: © Warren Goldswain/Shutterstock.com
© Aero-Imaging, Inc./Newscom, 64
© AP Images/Adam Bird, 49
© AP Images/Don Petersen, 21
© AP Images/Doug Hood/The Asbury Park Press, Doug Hood, 82
© AP Images/Frank Franklin II, 78
© AP Images/Seth Wenig, 45
© BSIP/Newscom, 61
© carlofranco/iStock.com, 22
© Christopher Peterson/Splash News/Newscom, 37
© David McNew/Getty Images, 11
© dem10/iStock.com, 54
© EHStock/iStock.com, 44
© fstop123/iStock.com, 32
© Gale, Cengage Learning, 50, 74
© gazmandhu/Shutterstock.com, 7
© GlobalStock/iStock.com, 40
© Horus-Images/Action Press/ZUMAPRESS.com, 16
© Jason Doiy/iStock, 80
© Joe Raedle/Getty Images, 73
© Kevin Dietsch/UPI/Newscom, 77
© Marc Romanelli/Getty Images, 13
© Nina Prommer/Patrick McMullan/Sipa USA via AP Images, 34
© Paul Conrath/Getty Images, 59
© Peter Macdiarmid/Getty Images, 18
© Randy Risling/Toronto Star via Getty Images, 26
© Rosebud Pictures/Getty Images, 57
© Shelley Wood/The Image Bank/Getty Images, 65
© Spencer Platt/Getty Images, 84
© Vidiriera/Shutterstock.com, 30
© William F. Campbell/The LIFE Images Collection/Getty Images, 70
© Yellow Dog Productions/Getty Images, 47

ABOUT THE AUTHOR

Toney Allman holds a BS in psychology from Ohio State University and an MA in clinical psychology from the University of Hawaii. She currently lives in Virginia and writes books for students on a variety of topics.